The Chakra Project

The Chakra Project

How the healing power of energy can transform your life

Georgia Coleridge

aster

An Hachette UK Company
www.hachette.co.uk

First published in Great Britain in 2018 by Aster,
a division of Octopus Publishing Group Ltd
Carmelite House, 50 Victoria Embankment
London EC4Y 0DZ
www.octopusbooks.co.uk

ISBN 9781912023233

A CIP catalogue record for this book is
available from the British Library.

Printed and bound in China.

10 9 8 7 6 5 4 3 2

Consultant Publisher Kate Adams
Art Director Yasia Williams-Leedham
Senior Editor Pollyanna Poulter
Copy Editor Mandy Greenfield
Designer Nicky Collings
Production Manager Caroline Alberti

Cover: front, Sharon Pittaway/Unsplash;
back, stilllifephotographer/Getty Images

Contents

Introduction

The human body is absolutely amazing. It is a miracle that a bundle of tiny cells has all the genetic instructions to turn into a fully grown, walking, talking, self-sufficient adult. In one lifetime it's estimated that our body will, on average, take 672,768,000 breaths and our hearts will beat an astonishing 3,363,840,000 times. But this incredible body is not just a clever machine; we also get the chance to fall in love, laugh and cry; to think, invent and explore; to communicate with each other, dream and create; even to ponder on the nature of reality, our soul and the divine.

The remarkable energy that makes all these things possible is called the life force, qi or prana. If DNA is the physical blueprint, then you could say that prana is the energetic blueprint that underpins and organizes it all. It is there, in every cell of our body, and it extends outside our body, too, creating an energy field or aura around us.

The earth has an energy field as well, which grounds us. We are also designed to absorb energy from sunlight and certain other wavelengths of light.

We pick up on all sorts of energy, all the time, at a vibrational level. Some people are sceptical about the idea of auras because they cannot see them, but the energy around you can alter your mood, cause physical symptoms and even warn you of danger. When you meet someone for the first time, you pick up many clues about them from their aura. You might click instantaneously or you might – for no obvious, logical reason – instinctively put up your guard. It is also your own energy field that reacts to places with a heavy, creepy atmosphere and tells you that you ought to leave.

You can also communicate energetically across long distances. Many people have had esoteric experiences that scientists really can't explain, such as thinking of a long-lost friend seconds before they telephone, or having the strong urge to contact someone you love at the very moment they are in danger.

What has all this got to do with chakras? In this book you will find out how chakras link our physical body with the energy around it. In this way, chakras affect every aspect of our lives. They are a reflection of our physical health, a guide to the deepest levels of our psyche, and our tools for spiritual growth and healing. They are both simple and profound, both practical and esoteric. Discovering more about them can radically change your life.

What are
Chakras?

Chakras are the interface between our hardworking physical body and the energy around us. In electrical terms, they act like a transformer between the two. As you may know, your laptop can't be plugged straight into the mains without blowing its circuit. It needs a special cable, with a transformer, to convert the current into a form it can use. You can think of prana as the life-force energy that runs through us, like electricity. And chakras are the transformers that connect our solid, physical laptop selves with the energy of our nonsolid layers.

You can also think of chakras as windows, or portals, between your physical body and your energy body. When they are working well, windows do an essential job, letting light and fresh air flow in and out of a building. If you closed your windows permanently, blocking the light with heavy curtains and piles of junk, your rooms would feel heavy, sick and airless. But if you left them open permanently, your rooms would feel unprotected and uncomfortable especially during hurricanes or icy weather. Healthy chakras – like healthy windows – need a good clean occasionally, so that they can let the energy in and out. If your chakras are unhealthy and have become jammed wide open or stuck shut, then they might need a major overhaul. This book will show you how to detect an unhealthy chakra and heal it.

SPIRALS AND SYMBOLS

In the ancient Indian Vedic scriptures the word "chakra" translates as "wheel". Chakras are usually depicted as spirals or circles of light. As they spin, chakras draw energy in and out of the body. Chakras connect the physical body with the emotional, mental and spiritual layers and can be visualized as many different discs or spirals stacked on top of one another. When they are spinning beautifully, energy flows.

Traditionally, each chakra can also be represented by a unique symbol known as a yantra. Based on lotus flowers, with different numbers of petals, they represent the qualities and associations of each chakra. You can see a simple version of these yantras at the beginning of each chapter.

COLOURS

Like a rainbow of light, each of the seven chakras is associated with a different colour: red, orange, yellow, green, blue, purple and a beautiful shining violet-white. Red is the slowest vibration and is connected with the base chakra between your legs. Violet-white is the highest colour vibration and is associated with the crown chakra at the top of your head. Between them, the other colours make up a beautiful rainbow bridge, connecting the earth and sky.

THE SPIRALS OF NATURE

Chakras are usually portrayed as spirals – an incredibly powerful symbol of spiritual growth. Our planet is part of the great spiral galaxy known as the Milky Way. And there are countless beautiful spirals in nature: twining plants that spiral upward; the Fibonacci sequence of spirals in the centre of a sunflower; the spiral fractals of shells or of Romanesco broccoli...Spirals can bring together opposing forces and lead them toward a place of unity. Once you start working on your chakras you may begin to notice spirals everywhere.

LOCATION

We have hundreds of chakras all over our body, including on the palms of our hands and the soles of our feet. In this book, we will focus on seven key chakras. The diagram *opposite* shows where these seven chakras can be found on your body.

ASSOCIATIONS

Each of the seven major chakras has different associations.

Of the lower chakras:

1 The base connects you to the earth and to your physical body.
2 The sacral is about physical pleasure and creativity.
3 The solar plexus is in charge of power.

Of the upper chakras:

4 The heart chakra is about love and compassion.
5 The throat expresses truth and communication.
6 The third eye is linked to intuition.
7 The crown is your connection with the divine.

Each chapter in this book will explore all these associations more deeply. The better you understand your chakras, the easier it is to look after them.

THE IMPORTANCE OF FLOW

The flow of energy through our chakras goes in two different directions. Each individual chakra draws energy in and out of itself, connecting our body and auric field with the outside world. All the chakras are also connected together vertically, to nourish and support each other. For a deeper explanation of these horizontal and vertical flows *see* the diagrams on pages 183 and 184.

Tuning into Energy: an exercise

Your hands are a great place to start to feel the kind of energy that flows through your chakras. You may be surprised at how effective this simple exercise is:

o Rub your hands together briskly and flex your fingers a few times.

o Hold your hands together in front of you, as though you are praying. Then slowly draw them apart.

o Bring your hands back together. As you do so, you will start to feel the energy between them. It might feel like the push of two magnets, repelling each other, or like a ball of energy you can cup between your hands.

o Draw your hands wider apart, then bring them together again. The energy will feel wider and bigger.

o Keep doing this and see how far apart you can go.

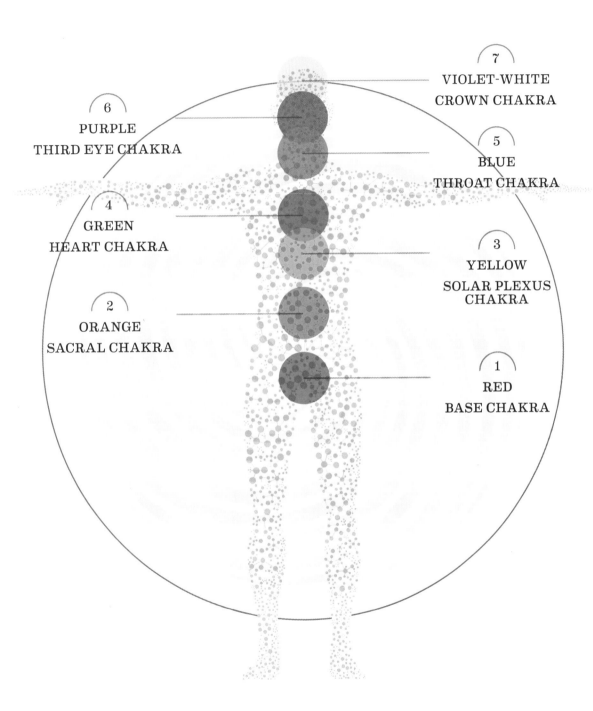

7
VIOLET-WHITE
CROWN CHAKRA

6
PURPLE
THIRD EYE CHAKRA

5
BLUE
THROAT CHAKRA

4
GREEN
HEART CHAKRA

3
YELLOW
SOLAR PLEXUS
CHAKRA

2
ORANGE
SACRAL CHAKRA

1
RED
BASE CHAKRA

How to Use
This Book

We'll start with an overall chakra health check, using a couple of different approaches to tune into your chakras and explore them. You will start to get a sense of where your chakras are in your body, how they feel and whether there are any particular areas to work on.

Then we'll focus on each of the seven main chakras in turn and get to know them better. They are each associated with a different beautiful rainbow colour, so it is easy to remember which one is which. Each chakra also has unique characteristics, so you will get a clear sense of how they look, feel and affect you in different ways.

When individual chakras are balanced they regulate the energy that comes in and out of your body, so that you feel healthy and energized but not overloaded. When all your chakras are balanced they work well together, like all the instruments in an orchestra, perfectly in harmony. But if any of your chakras is over- or under-active, it's like an orchestra with some instruments playing out of tune. Instead of harmony, there is cacophony. Your whole system can be under strain.

Should you find, when working through this book, that any of your chakras are unbalanced, there are plenty of suggestions to bring them back into harmony, including ways to strengthen and clear them (by removing stuck old energy from other people or from your past), as well as ways to protect them during a normal busy day. There are all sorts of different approaches, which range from practical suggestions you can try at home or work, to energy tecniques like breathing exercises and visualizations.

Finally, I'll show you ways to bring everything together so that you can work on all chakras together and deepen your connection. This process can be inspiring and energizing.

When I first started working on my own chakras I suddenly became much more aware of the beautiful shapes and colours they represent. The world seemed more exciting and colourful: I noticed beautiful fresh fruit and vegetables, flowers and spiral shapes all over the place. Energy really does flow where your thought goes.

By the end of the book your chakras will almost certainly be spinning more cleanly and your energy flowing better, both upward and downward. When you feel connected and all your chakras are working together, in a balanced way, you'll find it easier to evolve spiritually; you'll also breeze through the day-to-day challenges of being human.

A Note on Visualizations

If you have never done any energy work before, you might wonder whether the exercises in this book will work for you. Let me assure you that they definitely can. Try this little experiment now:

o Imagine picking up a very juicy, fresh lemon. Imagine how good it smells. Now imagine cutting it in half, bringing it up to your mouth, and slowly, slowly biting into it, letting the juice run over your tongue.

o Is your mouth watering just thinking about it?

How are your Chakras?

A Chakra
Health Check

We are going to start by scanning all your chakras, because these portals are crammed with information. A western doctor might take your blood pressure or listen to your chest with a stethoscope. A Chinese doctor might feel your pulses or look at your tongue. Either way, they are looking for clues about your health, so that they can diagnose and prescribe treatment.

As a healer, I am always looking for clues about my clients' energy, so I tune into each layer of their chakras with my hands. If their energy feels good, their physical health is likely to be good too. But if any part of their energy field feels toxic or suppressed, this can affect their immune system. Chakras work as a complete energy system: if just one of them is out of kilter, it can interrupt the energy flow of the whole system. But if you can find and fix it, then you can boost overall health and feel vibrant and fully alive.

Some of my clients' chakras feel blocked and heavy; others feel underpowered and faint, as though they have lost their glow. But holding my hand over a healthy chakra is a delight: when a chakra is spinning beautifully, it feels light and sparkly, like dust particles dancing in a beam of sunlight, or that wonderful feeling in the spring when you can sense that the sap is rising in the trees, the leaves are unfurling and the blossom is coming out.

When something good or bad has happened to clients in between sessions, it shows up in their chakras. And as we work on the chakras, week by week, their energy feels clearer. Even major life problems, or family issues that seemed overwhelming at our first session can be tackled, dismantled, healed and released, layer by layer.

It's easy for me to find patches of energy that need healing in my client's chakras. Under my hands they feel dense and out of place – like a heap of dirty washing in the middle of a perfectly tidy room. Why haven't they noticed for themselves? Sometimes it takes conscious effort. When you live with your own energy every day, you get used to it. Like a fish swimming in the ocean, your own body and energy field feel normal.

There are also parts that we don't want to feel: the shadows; the sharks cruising below the waterline of our conscious mind; old emotional wounds; painful family history; low-level physical pain. Most of us – consciously or unconsciously – block it all out, so that we can simply get on with our lives. But suppressing all these shadows can take a great deal of energy, like bicycling very hard with your brakes on – far more energy, in fact, than facing up to an issue and healing it. Physically, we may end up with rock-hard shoulders, stomach ulcers or insomnia. On an energetic level, chakras become distorted or blocked, which can make us feel dull and sluggish.

Over the next few pages, I'll take you through some simple visualizations to help you connect with your chakra energy. Try them with an open mind. There is no right or wrong way to explore your chakras. If you are more comfortable with words than images, you may find the detailed descriptions of your chakras at the beginning of each chapter are more helpful.

Assessing your Own Chakras

Here is a good place to start looking at your own chakras.

The Spiritual MRI Scan (*right*) and Lighthouse Meditation (*see* pages 22–3) are two different tecniques that can give you information, either visually or as a feeling in your body. Try one – or both – of them and you will find a method that will suit you.

You might find it helpful to record and play back these techniques (or get someone else to read them out loud), so that you can close your eyes, relax and immerse yourself fully.

TECHNIQUE 1

If you go for a full MRI scan in hospital, you lie inside a gleaming white tube, which scans your body from top to toe, using magnetic resonance. This is the spiritual version, that you can do comfortably at home. You may be surprised by how much you see or feel.

Spiritual MRI Scan

o Get some plain paper and pens or pencils. Draw a simple outline of your body and mark the location of the seven main chakras (you can use the diagram *opposite* as a guide).

o Lie down and close your eyes. Take some long, slow breaths. Imagine that a big beam of light is sweeping down your body like a spotlight, scanning you bit by bit, from the top of your head right down to the soles of your feet.

o As you imagine the light moving through you, be aware of images or sensations in each part of your body. If you are a visual person, you may see colours, shapes or patches of light and shadow with your inner eye. If you are more sensory (a feeler), you may notice areas of tingling, tightness, lightness, heaviness, soreness or changes of temperature.

o Keep breathing slowly and evenly. Scan yourself a second time, slightly more slowly, and see if you notice anything else.

o When you open your eyes, mark anything that you noticed on your drawing.

TECHNIQUE 2

When I was a child I visited a lighthouse. I'd never been in a building like it before and I found it fascinating, because it was so tall and thin. Each floor was a single room, stacked on top of the one below.

When you are standing or sitting, your energy body is a bit like a lighthouse: each chakra takes up a different floor, with each chakra colour on top of the one below.

In this visualization (which continues over the page) you take a journey to your own chakra lighthouse and walk into each room, for a really good look around.

If any of the rooms are overstuffed with furniture, feel cold or don't have working windows, it's a symbolic clue that you have a chakra that requires attention...

TECHNIQUE 2 CONTINUED

Lighthouse Meditation

o   Sit comfortably, with your back straight and your feet flat on the floor. Take some slow, deep breaths.

o   Imagine yourself on a beautiful hillside. You are alone, and you know this place is peaceful and safe. The sun is shining gently and you can feel the air on your face.

o   Look down at your feet. The hill slopes gently downward and there is a small, safe path. You follow it, one foot in front of the other. Notice that the path leads to a tall, thin lighthouse with windows. You feel drawn to it and want to explore it. It is safe for you to do so. The path leads to the front door.

o   Push open the door, close it behind you and let your eyes adjust to the light. You are in the **FIRST** room, which takes up the whole of the first floor. In the middle of the room is a **RED** candle, in a red holder, and a box of matches. Light the candle. Notice how the red light glows.

o   Look around. Turn and look at every wall. What do you notice about the room? Is it full or empty? Is there anything on the floor? Is there anything on the walls? Are there any pictures? Is it cool or warm? How clean is it? Look at the windows – do they let in light? Can you open them? How does this room make you feel? Stay here for a few more minutes.

o   Perhaps you hadn't seen it before, but there is a ladder leaning against one wall, leading up to a trapdoor in the ceiling. It is safe for you to climb it, rung by rung, one foot at a time. Push open the trapdoor, climb through safely and close it behind you. The floor is flat and very safe.

o   You are now on the **SECOND** floor. In the middle of the room is an **ORANGE** candle, in an orange holder, and a box of matches. Light the candle. Notice how the orange light glows. Look around as you did in the previous room, taking notice of how the room looks and feels. Stay here for a few more minutes before ascending the ladder again to the next floor.

o   You are now on the **THIRD** floor. In the middle of the room is a **YELLOW** candle, in a yellow holder, and a box of matches. Light the candle. Notice how the yellow light glows. Look around, taking notice of how the room looks and feels. Stay here for a few more minutes before ascending the ladder again to the next floor.

- You are now on the **FOURTH** floor. In the middle of the room is a **GREEN** candle, in a green holder, and a box of matches. Light the candle. Notice how the green light glows. Look around, taking notice of how the room looks and feels. Stay here for a few more minutes before ascending to the next floor.

- You are now on the **FIFTH** floor. In the middle of the room is a **BLUE** candle, in a blue holder, and a box of matches. Light the candle. Notice how the blue light glows. Look around, taking notice of how the room looks and feels. Stay here for a few more minutes before ascending to the next floor.

- You are now on the **SIXTH** floor. In the middle of the room is a **PURPLE** candle, in a purple holder, and a box of matches. Light the candle. Notice how the purple light glows. Look around, taking notice of how the room looks and feels. Stay here for a few more minutes before ascending to the next floor.

- You are now on the **SEVENTH** floor. This room is different from the others. It is the top of the lighthouse – the ceiling is made of glass. In the middle of the room is a pure **WHITE** candle, in a white holder, and a box of matches. Light the candle. Notice how the pure white light glows. Look around, taking notice of how the room looks and feels. How about the glass ceiling: how much light can come in?

- Perhaps you hadn't seen it before, but on one side of this room is the door to a lift, which goes slowly and gently down the outside of the building. Step into it and notice as, very slowly, it takes you down past the purple, blue, green, yellow and orange floors to the red floor. Step out of the lift onto the grass. Climb the path up the hill, back to where you started.

- Open your eyes. Make a note of anything you noticed in each of the rooms.

Some of the things you saw may be easy to interpret. Others may have a symbolic message that might require a little time until their meaning becomes clear to you.

The first time I did this visualization, my orange room looked like an L-shaped room in my grandfather's house. It was cluttered with toys, including my mother's old wooden rocking horse. The message was that I needed to clear family energy in the sacral chakra, both from my own childhood and from my mother's.

How to
Proceed?

Now that you are beginning to have a sense of your chakras, read the following seven chakra chapters for lots of ideas, exercises and pictures to inspire you further.

Starting at the base chakra, we will explore each chakra one by one. The better you know these energy portals, the easier you will find it to strengthen and heal them. Chakras work on so many different levels that this process can be powerful and life-changing.

You might find that you simply start noticing a lot more of those gorgeous chakra colours – it is amazing how beautiful the world is, once you start looking. If you like, take photos and post them on Instagram #ChakraProject. I would love to see them.

If your lower chakras need attention, you might decide to start moving your body more, by walking, dancing or taking up a yoga class. You might start eating more fresh, colourful food or powering through clutter and your "to do" lists.

If your heart requires attention, now is the time to clean up old wounds and blocks, nourish and protect it and change your vibration, so that you can both give and receive love.

If your upper chakras need attention, you might decide to visit a healer, clean up your energy field, take up singing lessons or set aside time for meditation.

You can start your chakra journey anywhere you like. Maybe you feel strongly inspired to jump straight to one particular chakra – perhaps one that already feels comfortable, or the one that you think is giving you the most trouble.

But for most people it feels solid and reassuring to start at the red base chakra and work upward to the crown (so this is how this book is arranged). This is like making sure that you construct really solid foundations before you build the rest of your house. If you are aiming to build a lighthouse with a very powerful beam, then good foundations are essential.

A Note on Intention

As you can see from the lemon exercise on page 12, energy flows where thought goes. Sometimes you only need to think about something and extraordinary things can start happening on a physical level (your mouth waters), on an emotional level (for example, when you think about someone you love) and, of course, your thoughts affect you all the time on an intellectual and spiritual level, too. This is why the exercises in this book can be extremely powerful if you approach them with intention.

Intention is a tool which can super-charge everything you do. It means setting up a particular thought or attitude in your mind. When you do, the universe often magically brings you what you are looking out for. If you do nothing else, when you read this book, set the intention to look out for the chakra colours, and see what starts to happen...

Base Chakra

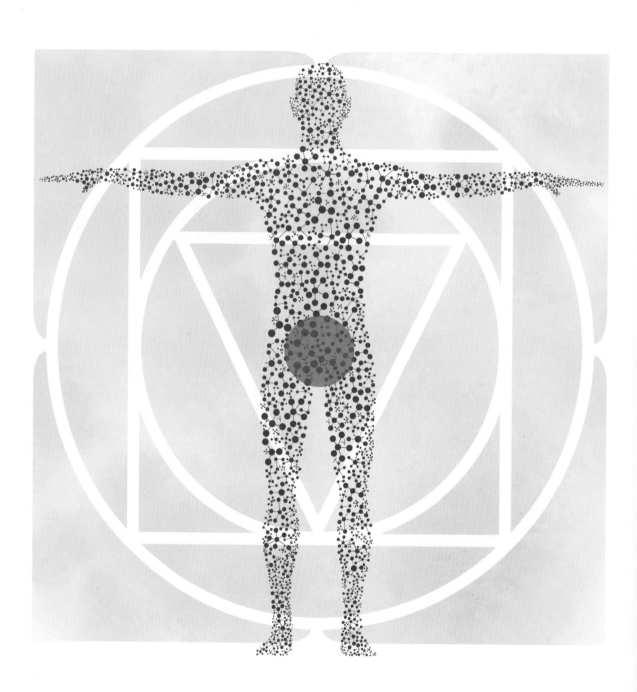

Ancient Sanskrit name	Muladhara (meaning: the root)
Commonly known as	Base chakra, root chakra, red chakra
Number	One, the first chakra
Location	Base of the spine, the perineum
Associations	Survival; the physical body; roots; connection to the earth, your body and your tribe
Related organs	Bones and skeleton, base of the spine, legs, feet, the large intestine, genitals
Sense	Smell
Element	Earth
Age	0–7 and 50–56
When in balance	Feeling grounded, satisfied and comfortable in your own skin; physically full of energy and in good health; living a stable life
When weak or damaged	Feeling spacey, ungrounded, anxious and unsatisfied; physically ill or weak; problems with the feet, legs, knees and/or bones, including sciatica; lower digestion issues, such as constipation and haemorrhoids
When over-developed	Being set in your ways; feeling physically stiff; hoarding; emotionally vulnerable to unexpected events
Symbol/yantra	A four-petalled lotus; the square in the middle represents the earth
Phrases	I am, I survive, I am safe, I have enough, I am grounded
Crystals	Try black, brown or red crystals, such as ruby, garnet and haematite, for grounding and protection

I am usually comfortable in my skin

I've got my tribe of family and friends

I enjoy the practical side of gardening

I enjoy moving and exercising my body

I have a good sense of smell

I love to be outdoors

I'm happy to be in a human body

I feel safe most of the time

My home feels safe and welcoming

There's enough money coming in to pay my bills

I have good physical energy

I enjoy my possessions and look after them

I enjoy walking barefoot

I'm a survivor; whatever happens, I will be fine

I can let go of clutter

I am Grounded

The base chakra is the wonderful, solid foundation for all the other chakras. Located at the base of the spine, in the perineum, it points downward, connecting us to the earth. A tall tree needs STRONG ROOTS to grow properly, while a tall building needs DEEP FOUNDATIONS to keep it stable. Our energy system is just the same: for strength, stability and the chance to soar spiritually, we need a solid base. The base chakra's other name is the root chakra, and when it is working well it keeps us grounded to the earth, so that our energetic roots can support and nourish us and keep us safe through the storms of life.

This is the most physical of all the chakras. This red chakra isn't about high ideals, deep thoughts or meditation; its main function is the SURVIVAL OF OUR PHYSICAL BODY. It takes us back to basics – to our ancestral, primeval needs: finding enough to eat and a safe shelter; maintaining the physical energy to hunt or forage; gathering and storing food and fuel for the winter; and staying on good terms with the rest of our tribe (because we wouldn't survive on our own).

Though we are no longer hunter-gatherers, these BASIC NEEDS are still strong, particularly when we are very young. Babies and small children need warmth, food and protection simply to survive. This chakra is particularly linked to the first seven years of life, including time inside the womb. If you had a happy (or at least uneventful) childhood, with LOVING parents, in a peaceful neighbourhood or a politically STABLE country, then you have a better chance than most of developing a healthy base chakra.

When the
Base
Chakra is Balanced

When this chakra is working well, life feels good. You feel SAFE AND GROUNDED. Your feet are firmly planted on the earth, and nothing much can upset your equilibrium.

You probably have good physical health and lots of vitality, with STRONG BONES, FEET AND LEGS. You might enjoy being out in nature, walking or gardening, or working outdoors with your hands. Your appetite may be good, and you can digest almost anything. You may have a deep visceral trust that everything will be all right, that your needs will be met and the EARTH is abundant enough to support you.

And you are good at MANAGING THE BASICS OF LIFE, possessing practicality and common sense. It may not be fancy, but there will be food in the cupboard. Even if you don't earn much, you can manage your money and pay your bills on time. You maintain your house, so that you don't need to worry about whether the windows lock properly or the rain will get in. You don't mind putting in the work to take care of unglamorous routine chores – you know that

cleaning, cooking, weeding the garden and DIY need to be done regularly, and it feels right to do so.

You may have strong links with your parents, siblings and extended FAMILY. If you have children, you take your responsibilities seriously; it feels natural to work hard to look after them. Even if you aren't close to your birth family, you find your tribe and can rely on your friends for mutual support and trust.

When the base chakra is spinning beautifully, it's the perfect launch pad to do all sorts of other exciting things, because when the basics of life are under control, you have resources and physical energy to spare. Your higher chakras may yearn to create, pursue a dream career, fall in love, write a novel or follow a spiritual path, and your base chakra can act as the SOLID PLATFORM to manifest all these dreams and make these wonderful things happen in a healthy way.

But when the base chakra is out of balance, it's another story. This chakra can be underpowered, overpowered or even a mixture of both.

Recognizing when the
Base
Chakra is Weak or Damaged

There are all sorts of reasons for a weak base chakra. Sometimes it's a question of not paying enough attention to your physical body – perhaps because you THINK TOO MUCH, or because you yearn for a spiritual connection. We are spirits in a human body, and this incarnation on earth is a tremendous opportunity to learn by experience. But if you FIND LIFE OVERWHELMING, it might feel safer to spend most of your time up in your head, or in the higher realms of your upper chakras.

On the surface it seems peaceful up there, but if you don't care for your physical body, you can get droopy, PHYSICALLY FRAGILE AND TIRED. If you don't look after the practical side of life – those boring chores, such as emptying the bins or paying the bills – your days can become messy and overwhelming. You can also seem flaky: full of good intentions that never seem to come to anything.

Your head can get you tangled up in knots, as you try to think or meditate your way out of problems. But if you would only listen to your body, the answer is often simple; when you get enough regular exercise, food, fresh air and sleep, many problems seem manageable and can even melt away.

The base chakra can also be damaged by traumatic events, particularly in childhood, when we soak up family trauma like sponges. But even as adults, it can be badly affected by losing a family member, being fired from your job, financial trouble, coping with serious illness, political instability or war. Even smaller events, such as moving house or even a long journey, can upset the base chakra.

When it's not spinning properly, you can feel UNGROUNDED. This is unsettling, like losing your grip, being unstable on your feet, chopped off at the knees, wrong-footed or feeling as if the rug has been pulled out from underneath you.

More than any others, this chakra can hold family energy. From your mother's emotions absorbed in the womb to ancestral memories of poverty, starvation, oppression or exile, these traumas can rumble under the surface and make you feel INEXPLICABLY WEAK, ungrounded and fearful.

Recognizing when the
Base
Chakra is Over-developed

When the base chakra is too large or spinning too fast, your system is like a tree with over-developed roots – there is no possibility of growth and change by transplanting yourself into soil that is more suitable.

With an over-developed base chakra, you can become almost too earthy, stuck in the mud and SET IN YOUR WAYS. Like a tree that can't bend in the wind, you might be physically stiff and unyielding. You hate to move house, for you literally feel uprooted.

If you've always done something a certain way (or generations of your family have), then you won't be open to any newfangled ideas, thank you very much. Your family and work colleagues might see you as a reliable, dependable rock, but secretly may find you a bit dull, with NO HIGHER SPARK to lighten your earthy common sense and practicality.

An INFLEXIBLE base chakra can also make you vulnerable. Because you are good at handling the physical world and are used to having life under control, you don't need much emotional flexibility, but unexpected events – such as a death in the family – can hit you harder than others.

WHAT HAPPENS TO OUR ENERGY FLOW IF THE BASE CHAKRA ISN'T BALANCED

If this chakra is underpowered, it can be hard to make projects actually happen. Energy might flow downward through the chakras and then get stuck. All sorts of kind thoughts, wonderful ideas or brilliant money-making schemes might be discussed, but somehow you never get around to sending that Get well card, writing that book or taking your business idea beyond the planning stage.

If the chakra is overpowered, it can be difficult to change or to feel deep satisfaction. When the basic drive to survive is working well, you may appear a success to the outside world, but if the energy doesn't flow upward, your success won't have the warmth of the heart connection or the divine spark of spiritual growth.

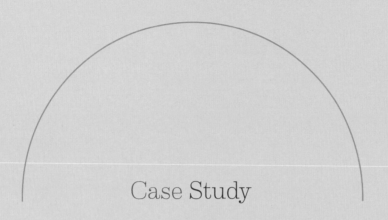

Case Study

WHEN THE BASE CHAKRA IS WEAK

Jane was a very pale young woman. She was anxious and felt depressed about her life. She said she felt indecisive and rootless. Her father was in the army, posted all over the world, so the family moved house 11 times and she was often the new girl in class at school.

She was accepted by a prestigious English university to study law, but gave it up after less than two years and moved to Berlin to study German, which she had learned as a child. A few months later she moved to London and switched degrees again. Jane now wanted to be a psychologist, but the enormous reading list made her head ache, and she kept changing her mind about whether or not to move back to continental Europe.

The energy in her base chakra felt very faint, as though it hadn't really developed properly. Energetically, she didn't have good, healthy roots. Although change had felt uncomfortable during

her childhood, it also felt normal for her. I did some inner-child work with her, healing incidents when she had been uprooted to different houses, countries and schools, and she practised grounding exercises (for details of both of these, *see* pages 44 and 64).

My recommendations were practical ones – about creating roots for herself now. At a basic level, I suggested that she would feel better if she scrubbed her room, painted the walls and hired an industrial carpet-cleaning machine. A walk every day would help to clear her head and connect her with her body. Jane wouldn't be able to compete financially with her law-school friends, but a temporary job (however lowly) would bring in more money, until she qualified. This helped to lift Jane's mild depression and she completed her degree.

How to Heal the
Base Chakra

In this section you will find all sorts of ideas to heal, strengthen and balance your base chakra. These include focusing on colour, food and your physical body, improving aspects of your life associated with this chakra and, finally, a meditation to connect you with your energetic roots.

Each of the chakra chapters in this book will then follow a similar pattern but the base chakra is the foundation for them all.

This chakra governs our solid, physical day-to-day life. We could spend decades working on ways to balance this chakra: getting our finances in shape, creating somewhere great to live, taking care of our health, getting fit, eating properly and sorting out family relationships. Please don't panic! These are all only suggestions, so pick out a few that you like the sound of and see where they take you. Whatever you choose, you'll be helping your base chakra and beginning the task of cleaning and lightening your entire energy system.

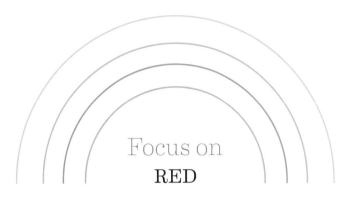

Focus on
RED

The base chakra is linked to a beautiful warm, vibrant red. Colour psychologists say the vibration of this colour is very energizing. But there are all sorts of other gorgeous hues across the red spectrum that might appeal to you, ranging from dark burgundy and earthy reddish brown to zingy magenta and soft, light pink.

Look out for red: the more you seek out this colour, the more you will notice it. Each time you do, it's a reminder to focus on your base chakra. See how many red things you can pick out at home and on the street: a bowl of raspberries, red flowers in the park, red lipstick and pink cheeks, a snazzy red sports car. Once you start looking, red will start popping up everywhere.

Wear something red: start with something small (and give yourself double location points for red socks or red underwear), or put a red tag on your bunch of keys, so that you see it every time you come home.

You could make a little altar, with red flowers and other red objects. Or post pictures of red items on social media. This is all about using the colour as a visual cue, to focus your intention on this chakra.

Feed your
Base Chakra

Every time you eat red food – even an ordinary tomato salad or a spoonful of tomato sauce – you can set the intention to use its wonderful colour to ground and nourish your base chakra. You might be surprised how much red food you notice when you focus on this area. Other vegetables to look out for include red peppers, chilies and red lettuce leaves, such as radicchio.

There are also many varieties of red fruit: you may become aware of seeing more strawberries, raspberries, cranberries, mulberries, redcurrants and ruby red pomegranates than before. Lots of fruit comes in beautiful shades of red, including rosy apples, pears, peaches, nectarines, rhubarb, red grapes and blood oranges.

The base chakra means "root", so while you are focusing on this area, also look out for root vegetables of any colour. Energetically, it helps that they grow in the ground, and there is something particularly comforting and earthy about them. Try eating more potatoes (especially red-skinned ones), sweet potatoes, carrots, parsnips, turnips, celeriac, yams, garlic and ginger. Red onions, beetroot and radishes get double root chakra points.

Heal your
Physical Body

One of the most obvious ways to balance your base chakra is through your physical body.

Your body gives you valuable clues about your health, but it's far too easy to block out its messages until you are really ill or in pain. This is an opportunity to pay attention to what your body has to say. Book a massage: which areas are reminding you that they feel tender? Sign up for a yoga class: which muscles complain as you stretch? Pay attention during the day: when do you feel thirsty and what food is your body craving?

BOOK A BODY HEALTH CHECK

Thinking about going for a checkup? Now is a good time, particularly for your feet, legs and the base of your torso. Seize the initiative and get help for your bunions, verruca or athlete's foot. Clicking knee? Book a physiotherapy appointment. Don't be embarrassed to ask your regular doctor about a cervical smear test, prostate examination or recurring haemorrhoids (doctors see base-chakra body parts all the time).

GET MOVING

A sedentary indoor life – commuting, working on our computers, checking our mobiles – isn't good for our base chakra. If you feel tired and lethargic you might feel tempted to spend even more time in front of the television, but your whole body would probably feel better if you could add more physical movement into your day instead. Moving your body pumps oxygenated blood around your system, relaxes your muscles and fascia and helps your energy to flow, too.

Perhaps the easiest way to exercise is to add some walking into your routine. Take the stairs instead of the lift, or use your feet for short journeys instead of the car. Even ten minutes' occasional walking is better than nothing. And if you get ambitious, there are plenty of apps that can tell you how many steps you have done.

CONNECT WITH YOUR FEET

Your feet – like your base chakra – connect you with the ground. Try massaging your feet, or book some professional reflexology to move the focus of your energy from your head to the lowest part of your body.

Walk barefoot around the house as often as you can. Even better, try to walk in bare feet outdoors on the grass or on a sandy beach.

You can even connect yourself energetically with the planet on tarmac, in shoes. A good and simple mini-meditation is to remind yourself occasionally to think about the soles of your feet as they touch the ground. For extra grounding, imagine that you have energetic roots coming from your feet (for more on roots, *see* page 44).

Tune into your
Base
Chakra

The base chakra is all about having a safe, stable environment. This section has suggestions on connecting with nature, then getting your home running well and your finances in shape.

CONNECT WITH NATURE

The base chakra connects us to the earth – the incredible giant planet on which we live – and to the living plants and animals upon it. To feed your base chakra, get as much nature into your life as you can.

- Walk, often.

- Eat your lunch in the park.

- Photograph flowers for Instagram, and bring them home to put in a vase.

- Grow plants; getting your hands into the earth is particularly good for the base chakra. Even if you haven't got a garden, you can grow herbs and tomatoes on your windowsill.

- Sit with your back against a big tree and feel the soothing, grounding energy against your spine. Imagine connecting with the sap flowing from the roots into the trunk. (You could also hug the tree, if you are feeling keen.)

- Lie flat on a lawn or in a field and feel the earth beneath your back.

- Go camping or on a hiking trip – this is a very base-chakra holiday, walking and sleeping in nature; it also brings you up close and personal with all sorts of basic bodily needs that we take for granted.

- Pick wild blackberries or visit a pick-your-own farm.

- Buy a pet, or borrow someone's dog for weekend walks.

- Hang out with small children. Perhaps because they are so much closer to the ground, they find beetles, earwigs, ducks and dandelions infinitely fascinating. Let them remind you how to play in a sandpit, jump in a muddy puddle or collect stones and shells on the beach.

- Bury your nose in the petals of flowers, because the base chakra is also linked to the sense of smell. Before you eat beautiful fruit and vegetables, smell the zest and the juice. And of course appreciate the lovely smell of fresh, clean earth.

GET ORGANIZED

Making your home more comfortable can affect your base chakra, although this is all about the basics rather than fancy decor. If your home is fundamentally organized and under control (so that you don't unexpectedly run out of clean underwear or spend ages every morning looking for your car keys), life runs more smoothly. Because of our primeval survival instinct, you are also more likely to get a good night's sleep in a calm, safe place.

How to tackle it

If your home feels out of control (perhaps because you've got small children, spend a lot of time at work or aren't particularly interested in being a domestic god or goddess) and this is starting to bother you, you may not know where to start. If you are feeling ungrounded, then an untidy house or a long "to do" list can seem overwhelming. Either of these two methods can kick-start your lethargy into action:

o   Begin with the very smallest job.

o   Begin with the bugbear (the job that is annoying you the most).

Starting small could mean narrowing your focus, to something you know you can do. Can't face that giant pile of admin? Start by cleaning out your wallet or handbag. Kitchen looks like a bombsite after the weekend? Wash one saucepan, or take out one bag of rubbish. Once you've got going, you may find that it's not so hard to carry on.

Starting with the bugbear means focusing on that annoying problem and making it your priority to solve it. Does your family run around like headless chickens every morning looking for coats and school bags? Make a concerted effort to put up some coat hooks. Each time you solve a bugbear, small or large, the rest of your life will feel more stable.

FACE UP TO CLUTTER

If you have a lot of clutter and find it hard to tackle, this could definitely be a base-chakra issue. It can date back to that old fear that the earth is not abundant and you had better hold on to what you've got – just in case. This may hark back to a difficult childhood or a traumatic event in your life that you don't want to look at. Or you may have absorbed ancestral fears from parents or grandparents who lived through a war or other displacement.

You can start to tackle clutter by beginning small: one item at a time; but if the process brings up lots of fear, you may need to do some deeper healing work on yourself.

TAKE CONTROL OF YOUR FINANCES

Money is also a base-chakra issue, and it helps to have a good relationship with it. If you are scared to open your bank statement, have only a hazy idea what you spend, splurge or hoard money, deny yourself or your family basic items that you can afford or worry excessively about never having enough, this is the time to take stock. Almost everyone in the world would like to have more money. But when the base chakra is working well and you feel grounded, it's easier to manage what you have, easier to ask for a raise, easier to prioritize what you spend and easier to budget for your future.

Get useful advice from books, articles and savvy friends on managing your money and budgeting. Your matter-of-fact, practical base chakra would also tell you it is never too early to start putting money aside for your pension (unlike your pleasure-seeking sacral chakra, which might prefer to splurge on a holiday or sports car – more about this later).

If the thought of opening the Pandora's box of your finances brings up strong emotions – particularly fear – then you may need to do some deeper healing around this issue.

Base Chakra Meditation

FINDING YOUR ROOTS

I often use this visualization at the end of healing sessions to ground and protect my clients. I like working directly with the feet, but you can also visualize roots coming straight from your base chakra.

o Close your eyes and imagine a beautiful big tree. Look at the trunk and the texture of the bark. Look up at the spread of branches: the large limbs, the smaller branches, the twigs and leaves. Now look down at the ground, where you can see the top of the roots that go into the earth. These roots nourish the tree, with water and nutrients. They keep it strong and stable. If you could look under the ground, you would see how deep and wide these roots grow – a beautiful network spreading into the earth.

o With this thought in your mind, you are going to reconnect with your own human, energetic roots. Bring your attention down to your feet and breathe OUT. With each OUT breath, allow your feet to feel heavier. Now imagine that the energy of each OUT breath is flowing down from the soles of your feet through the floor, through any rooms below and then happily deep into the earth. As you travel down with this OUT breath, it is like sending a root deep underground. With each OUT breath, more and more roots are created, spreading deep, spreading wide. Notice as you see, hear or feel your energetic roots spreading deep in the earth. With each OUT breath, go to the tip of the roots, so that they spread even deeper and wider. Keep breathing until the network is strong.

o Now use your IN breath, too, to pull the lovely rich earth energy up into your feet. On your OUT breath, go back to the tip of the roots. With your next IN breath, bring the earth energy up to your knees – and so on, flowing slowly up your body, until you are full of beautiful, grounding earth energy.

o When you have finished, thank the earth energy and slowly open your eyes.

CONNECTING TO YOUR ANCESTORS

Our ancestors are our roots to the past. Their fears and experiences, as well as blessings, can affect all of our chakras, particularly the base. By acknowledging ancestors, you can help to heal family energy. Start by collecting names, stories and photographs from relatives or from genealogical websites. Perhaps set up a little ancestor altar, with photographs. Send them loving thoughts and prayers. But also set the intention to release ancestral energy that is not yours from your body. (See bibliography on page 189 for more information.)

Sacral
Chakra

Ancient Sanskrit name	Svadhishthana (meaning: sweetness; one's own abode)
Commonly known as	Sacral chakra, lower belly chakra, orange chakra
Number	Two, the second chakra
Location	Lower belly, lower back
Associations	Physical pleasure; fully experiencing the emotions; flowing movement; sexuality; creativity; the moon
Related organs	Lower back, pelvic area, intestines, reproductive organs, bladder, kidneys
Sense	Taste
Element	Water
Age	8–14 and 57–63
When in balance	Able to feel pleasure; take joy in life; accepting of change and going with the flow; happy with your sexuality
When weak or damaged	Numb in the body; lack of appetite; emotionally cold and distant; fear of change; sense of isolation; ashamed of your physical appearance; sexual denial; physically stiff
When over-developed	Riding a rollercoaster of emotions; blocked creativity; physical problems in the pelvic area; addiction; selfishness
Symbol/yantra	A six-petalled lotus; the crescent represents the moon
Phrases	I feel, I am joyful, I create, I move, I flow, I experience
Crystals	Try orange crystals, such as orange carnelian, calcite, citrine or aventurine to amplify your life force

I've got a good gut instinct

My lower digestion works pretty well

I find it easy to get stuck in and let my creative juices flow

I notice when the phases of the moon affect me

I enjoy being spontaneous

I enjoy being touched or massaged

I like spending time in or near water

I like to use my hands to do or make things

I have hobbies and projects on the go, which bring me pleasure

I drink plenty of water

Strong emotions are great – part of being alive

I don't expect my life to go in a straight line; the flow of life is more creative than that

Life is fun

I can be playful

I enjoy sex

I am Experiencing

A healthy sacral chakra is like a delicious orange – full of sweetness and juice.

Like the base chakra, the sacral is connected to your physical body and life force, but its focus has progressed from survival to the sheer JOY OF BEING ALIVE. As you move up into this orange chakra, everything gets more fun and juicy.

In the base chakra, you stick with your tribe for duty and safety, but in the sacral it's about choosing to spend time with other people, for PLEASURE; about noticing and enjoying the taste, smell, colour and variety of the food you eat; about SENSUOUS ENJOYMENT and INTIMACY.

The sacral chakra also connects you with the joy of MOVEMENT, FLOW, CHANGE AND SPONTANEITY. It is linked to the moon, and its element is water; lunar waxing and waning and tidal ebb and flow are both good symbols of the constant motion of this chakra and the way it stretches your bandwidth of experience.

This chakra is located in the lower belly, between your navel and your pubic bone. Like all the middle chakras, it projects both forward (from your stomach) and backward (from the small of your back). It covers the physical area of your intestines, bladder, kidneys and womb. This part of the body can EXPERIENCE THINGS INTENSELY, on both a physical and emotional level. Visceral feelings, rumbling low in the belly, are very different to emotions in the heart or upper chakras. Because the womb is in this area, the sacral chakra is also associated (even for men) with a deep, instinctive CREATIVITY and the gestation of projects.

This chakra's Sanskrit name is Svadhishthana, which can be translated as both "sweetness" and "one's own abode". The sacral chakra is strongly linked to the ages of 8–14 years – a time when a child can roam a little more freely, discovering the joys of the world for himself or herself.

When the
Sacral
Chakra is Balanced

When your sacral chakra is working well, life is full of joy. You feel ENERGETIC, and OPTIMISTIC about the next delight coming your way. You seek out pleasurable experiences and can even find the fun in routine chores. Like a healthy, happy child, you are comfortable in your body and can open yourself up to appreciate each moment.

Life seems to flow easily and well for you; you can manage the basic chores partly because you have enough stimulation and variety to keep you interested. You may ENJOY NEW CHALLENGES at work, new friends, new books or new projects. Somehow they don't overwhelm you – they give you energy.

You are also INSTINCTIVELY CREATIVE. You can throw together a delicious meal without much effort, and it's not a problem if extra guests turn up unexpectedly. You may dress creatively, intuitively choosing unusual combinations and colours that suit you. You have a knack for making rooms feel welcoming and beautiful, by adding colour or fresh flowers. You might enjoy making things with your hands, or painting. You also appreciate other people's creative endeavours, and enjoy visiting galleries, museums or the theatre – anything that is more beautiful or intense than normal life.

You enjoy spending time with other people and have SATISFYING FRIENDSHIPS. You are happy having a cup of tea with a friend, but you also love a good party. Your love life is another source of pleasure, and you are COMFORTABLE WITH YOUR SEXUALITY.

Because you enjoy moving your body, you may be graceful and have LOTS OF PHYSICAL ENERGY. If your job doesn't give you much scope to move, you might go for a walk at lunchtime, or swimming in the evening, for the sheer pleasure of stretching out. Because your body is fit and flexible, you can handle the extremes of strong emotion.

But when the sacral chakra is out of balance, life can seem either dry and dull (lacking juice) or intense and overwhelming. This chakra can be underpowered, overpowered or even a mixture of both.

Recognizing when the
Sacral
Chakra is Weak or Damaged

When your sacral chakra isn't spinning well, life isn't much fun at all. You might feel flat, numb or even slightly depressed. There's not much joy or colour – NOTHING TO LOOK FORWARD TO. You might work hard because you have to, but you're just getting through the days. You don't care what you eat. Seeing friends and family is a duty. Sex is simply another chore. You might seem EMOTIONALLY COLD AND DISTANT. You turn down invitations and make excuses not to see people.

The sacral chakra is strongly linked to movement. If you DON'T MOVE ENOUGH, it's hard to process strong emotions and allow them to flow through the body. If these emotions build up, and feel overwhelming, this chakra can become gummed up and stagnant.

There are numerous reasons for a weak sacral chakra. Sometimes we are just busy and barely have energy for anything beyond the basics. This can happen if you have a lot of OUTSIDE PRESSURE: a heavy workload, a house move, a new baby or stressful family events. And all these things are worse if you aren't feeling well or don't sleep properly.

But sometimes the pressure comes from INSIDE. You might be replaying old scripts that make you avoid opportunities for joy and relaxation. These are often the words of authority figures – parents, teachers or bosses – who told you to STOP PLAYING, KEEP WORKING and squashed your natural capacity for joy. If you internalize them, their words can become your own.

Any kind of traumatic event in the family can affect a child's sacral chakra. If my clients have divorced parents, they often hold a lot of stuck energy in this area. Some is their own unprocessed reaction to the situation; some is their parents' rage and pain.

The most serious example of sacral-chakra invasion is any kind of sexual abuse, particularly in children. Abuse can affect all the chakras, but it's particularly relevant for this one because it can SHUT DOWN your capacity to feel.

Sometimes people have a weak sacral chakra because they are ASHAMED OF THEIR PHYSICAL BODY and would rather not engage with it. They may feel they are too ugly, fat or thin – or just a strange shape. They may have been told that sex is dirty, or been shamed as a child for wetting themselves. If they were less sporty or more clumsy than other children, they may have been yelled at in a sports class for being slow or missing a ball.

Recognizing when the
Sacral Chakra is Over-developed

When this chakra is too large or spinning too fast, you might feel as though you NEVER GET ANY PEACE. You may feel things so intensely in your body that it's like being in a little boat at sea: one minute up on a wave of joy, the next plunged into a trough of ANXIETY or DESPAIR. The sacral chakra is meant to bring us to the extremes of human experience. If we don't experience emotions and problems, then we can't grow, but if this chakra is spinning too fast, the flow of energy feels OUT OF CONTROL.

Just as dangerous: you might be so ADDICTED TO PHYSICAL SENSATION that you find yourself eating or drinking too much, driving dangerously, maxing out on your credit cards or sleeping with people you don't know or like. Or you might be ADDICTED TO CHANGE, feeling bored and unhappy unless you constantly switch jobs, find new partners or take yourself back onto the road.

If this chakra is really dominant, you can become incredibly SELFISH. Your own pleasure comes first, and you don't care how anyone else feels. In extreme cases this can even result in someone becoming a sexual predator (though this kind of behaviour can also be a solar plexus chakra issue about power).

WHAT HAPPENS TO OVERALL FLOW IF THE SACRAL CHAKRA ISN'T BALANCED?

If this chakra is underpowered, the other lower chakras – the base and solar plexus – are like a dry sandwich with no filling. Everything is all work and no play.

If the chakra is overpowered, the higher chakras can't do their job properly. If you get stuck in physical pleasure-seeking, it's harder to experience the higher delights, such as the joy of falling in love or your connection to the divine.

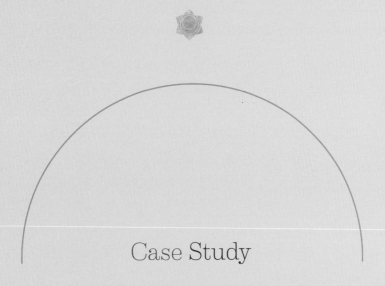

Case Study

WHEN THE SACRAL CHAKRA IS IN SHOCK

The year that Jim's mother died, his wife also left him, and the pain was so intense that he started drinking to numb his feelings. He just about managed to stay sober during work hours, but in the evenings he often went out to bars, and sometimes woke up the next morning with a splitting hangover and a stranger in his bed.

He couldn't bear to pack up his mother's house. And he couldn't face going back to his old flat to pick up his own books and possessions. His new flat was empty and soulless – a place to keep his clothes, and nothing much else.

His wake-up call was a hiking holiday with two old friends. He assumed they would spend most of their time drinking around the campfire, but it was actually three days of walking in the wilderness, and the alcohol ran out on the first day.

As he walked, with no alcohol to numb the pain, Jim found himself sobbing about his mother and his broken marriage. His shocked friends persuaded him to sign up to Alcoholics Anonymous when he got home, and begged him to see a therapist. He still doesn't like talking about his feelings, but Jim is beginning to explore them now, and he is still sober.

How to Heal the
Sacral Chakra

Working with the sacral chakra can be a lot of fun. This is the opportunity to give yourself permission to enjoy relaxing massages, take long, indulgent baths and focus on the hobbies and activities you enjoy.

If a voice in your head is telling you that you really don't have time for this kind of thing, recognize that it is probably a puritanical old script. Ask it to move aside while you block out time in your diary for activities that you relish. The following suggestions are meant to be a pleasure, not a chore, and there is no pressure to work through them all.

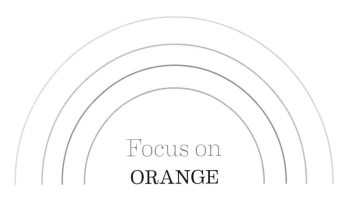

Focus on
ORANGE

The sacral chakra is linked to the colour orange – a dazzling, zingy colour, like the fruit itself. There are all sorts of other hues across the orange spectrum that might also appeal to you, ranging from salmon pink to coral, amber and saffron.

Each time you notice orange, it's a little reminder to focus on your sacral chakra. So see how many orange things you can spot during a normal day: from someone in the street with flaming Titian hair to a gorgeous sunset.

Wear something orange, even if it is a small item, such as an orange scarf (double points for anything slung over the hips). You could also put some orange soap in the bathroom (to remind you of the link with the element of water) or orange flowers in your bedroom (to represent sensuousness).

You could make a little altar or post pictures of orange items on social media, to focus your intention on this chakra.

Feed your
Sacral Chakra

● When you eat any orange food, set the intention to use its beautiful glowing colour to balance your sacral chakra.

Look out for orange fruit: the citrus family of course, including satsumas and clementines. Other orange fruit includes kumquats, apricots, mangoes, peaches, nectarines, papaya, cape gooseberries, cantaloupe melons and persimmons.

For vegetables, try looking out for orange peppers, sweet potatoes, pumpkins and butternut squash; plus orange spices such as turmeric, ground coriander and paprika.

As this chakra governs our intestines, you could also try eating fermented vegetables. Each mouthful can contain trillions of good bacteria which help to support your gut. Try live sauerkraut or kimchi from a health-food shop; you can even make your own (there are entertaining instructions on YouTube).

As the sacral chakra is paired with the sense of taste, try appreciating every mouthful. As well as giving you pleasure, eating your food mindfully is good for your digestive system.

As this chakra is so strongly associated with water, also try drinking extra glasses of it during the day (for more on this, *see* page 60).

Heal your
Physical Body

Being kind to your physical body is a good way to connect with your sacral chakra.

PAMPER YOURSELF

If you suddenly found you were very rich and had unlimited time, what would you do to bring more pleasure into your life?

I love being massaged, but for a long time I hardly ever booked myself in for one. It seemed too, well, indulgent for normal life. I started booking a massage or two when I was working on my own sacral chakra. Now, it is part of my monthly routine. You might prefer to have a reflexology appointment, head massage, hot shave, manicure, facial or a blow-dry. Or to sit in a hot tub, sauna or steam room. If money is tight, you could always try massaging your own hands, feet or stomach.

If you have a poor body image, try thanking your body for all the kind things it does for you, and focus on the parts that you do like.

LOOK AFTER YOUR BELLY

Although it may not actually make you feel pampered, if you pay attention to the organs in the sacral chakra area, they will feel happier.

A good start is to adjust your food, for a happy gut; drink more water, for a healthy bladder and kidneys; and if you are female, cut down on sugar and build in some relaxation, to help regulate your monthly hormones.

ENJOY MOVING YOUR BODY

It could be yoga, a dance class, tennis, golf, rock climbing, a martial art, 5Rhythms, clubbing or shaking a tail feather at your cousin's wedding – it doesn't matter what it is, as long as you move and you enjoy it (double points for belly dancing and martial arts that make you concentrate on your lower belly, and for swimming and making love).

(For more on swimming, making love and chakra yoga, see pages 60, 63 and 176.)

BELLY BREATHING

This is a remarkably simple technique to bring movement to your sacral chakra area. It is good for your digestive system and very calming for your entire body.

1 Lie down somewhere comfortable.

2 Put your hands on your lower stomach.

3 As you take slow, deep breaths, allow your lower stomach to rise and fall. You will know when you are doing the correct movement because your hands will gently rise and fall with each breath.

Once you've got the knack, you can do this anywhere, in any position.

Tune into your
Sacral Chakra

● This chakra is connected to the element of water and to the cycles of the moon. This section is also about tuning into this chakra to amplify its joy, spontaneity and creativity.

FIND JOY IN WATER

Humans are made up of water – 70 percent of our body (and even more in children) – and have a primeval connection with water, from the days when our ancestors first crawled out of the ocean. Water is vital for life and is incredible, magic stuff. Without it, plants can't grow and we can't survive.

In psychology, water can represent our emotions. The animal connected to the sacral chakra is a crocodile-like creature called a Makara, which has the ability to dive down deep into our unconscious and then come back up to the surface with insights.

Every time you encounter water, it's a good reminder of your scaral chakra and of its qualities of movement and flow. Here are some ways water can heal and balance your sacral chakra:

o Surfing on giant waves in Hawaii would be ideal. But wild swimming, paddling in the sea, walking alongside a river, feeding the ducks in the park or just splashing through puddles is good, too.

o Next time you are in the bath or shower, try to be aware of how the water feels on your skin, how it flows and ripples, how the light passes through it.

o Even when you simply turn on a tap remember how blessed we are to have water.

o For a chakra shower cleanse, *see* page 171.

OBSERVE THE MOON

The moon represents an important aspect of the sacral chakra. Its constant movement – the waxing and waning – is associated with the duality within us, the ebb and flow between yin and yang, light and dark, left and right, up and down, movement and stillness, masculine and feminine. A healthy sacral chakra can joyfully hold together the two polarities within us.

A simple way to raise awareness of this is to observe the cycles of the moon and notice what effect it has on you physically, and what emotions it brings up within you.

MAKE LOVE

This is a good opportunity to focus on your love life and reconnect with joy and intimacy. If your sexuality is fearful or frozen, find a healer or therapist whom you trust. As well as healing your sacral chakra, you may need to work on your base chakra and heart chakra.

HAVE FUN

Whatever constitutes your idea of fun, just go for it! Watch some funny movies. Meet up with your warmest, most entertaining friends. Go to the seaside for the day, or to a theme park with wild rides. Do something you enjoyed as a child – such as cycling, flying a kite or eating cake dough out of the bowl. Hang out with small children or friendly dogs. And remember to smile.

BE CREATIVE

If you come from a creative family, were encouraged at school and have a strong sacral chakra, being creative might come naturally to you. But if your parents didn't like noise or mess, or if your teachers told you that you were bad at writing or art, then your sacral chakra might still be dented and a little shy about expressing itself.

If you are drawn to a creative project, but feel intimidated, remind yourself that it is perfectly okay to start small. You may not be able to draw well now, but focus on what you can do and work from there. Do you already doodle circles or stickmen? Have you ever looked hard at the structure of a flower, or at shafts of sunlight coming through a window? If you enjoy any of those things, give yourself permission to explore further.

If you feel you would like to write a book, but the idea is daunting, again start small and suspend your judgment. Could you sit and dream in the bath, and see where your ideas take you? Try spending 15 minutes simply writing, without stopping to edit it, and see where it gets you. It's about giving yourself permission and taking the first step.

I never thought of myself as a visually creative person, because I was so bad at drawing and painting at school. But working with chakras gave my creativity a huge boost. I started posting chakra pictures on Instagram, and suddenly I was seeing colours and shapes everywhere – my brain was buzzing with creative ideas.

ENJOY BEING ALIVE

Here is a further list of suggestions to boost your creativity and *joie de vivre*. You could get creative yourself, of course, and come up with a whole lot more ideas.

o Enjoy having flowers in your home – they don't have to be for special occasions, and neither do candles or your good china.

o Pin up postcards that inspire you on the refrigerator or above your computer.

o Add some colour to your home, starting with something small that makes you feel happy.

o Put together different combinations of clothes (and don't save your best clothes for special occasions).

o Buy an adult colouring book and a great set of pens.

o Sign up for an art class – it's never too late to learn to paint, throw pots or make furniture.

o Hang out with creative friends, and visit galleries to inspire you.

Sacral Chakra Meditation

MEETING YOUR INNER CHILD

This visualization is a good way to connect with parts of yourself that are stuck and frozen, particularly aspects of yourself from childhood that need help. I often use this with my healing clients and they find it very powerful.

- Start by grounding your body. Take some long, slow belly breaths and, as you exhale, allow each part of your body to relax, beginning with your feet and working upward. Your head can stay as wide awake as it likes but, using your breath, allow your body to feel heavy and relaxed. Ask your guides and guardian angels to stand with you, to help and protect you.

- Now take yourself back to the place where you lived as a child. Stand outside and notice the colour and shape of the front door. You are setting this up so that the journey is extremely safe. Your inner child will recognize you, feel the connection and know that you are a safe person who has come to help.

- As you go up to the front door, your inner child opens it. They are pleased to see you. That connection is there. They take you by the hand and you walk into the house. You recognize the colours and shapes. Your inner child takes you to the bedroom and shows you their toys and books. You recognize them. Sit down and play with them together.

- After a while your inner child starts to feel sleepy and comes close to you. You are also relaxed and quite tired and your inner child knows that you will listen to anything they have to say. Let your inner child tell you all their worries or concerns. You might hear the words, or they might whisper them silently in your ear.

- Your inner child has been in that house on their own for a long time. Tell them that you understand how hard it has been. Say that if they like, they can come and live with you, in your heart. The two of you would be stronger and happier together. If your inner child agrees (and this may not happen), feel the boundary between the two of you dissolve, until you are the same person.

- Imagine filling the room and then the house with light. As you walk out of the door, you see another doorway that leads you back into your current life. Walk through it, back into your body and gently open your eyes.

Solar Plexus Chakra

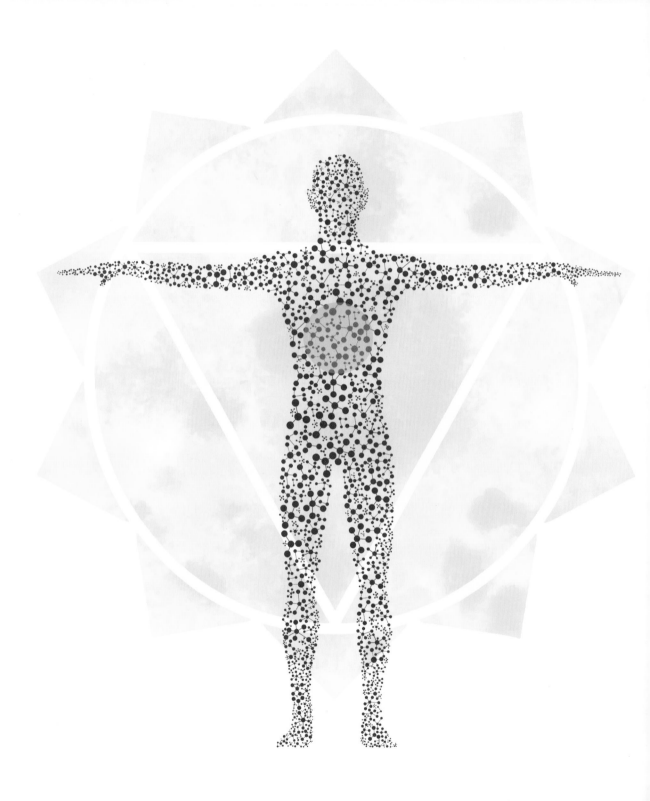

Ancient Sanskrit name	Manipura (meaning: lustrous gem)
Commonly known as	Solar plexus chakra, navel chakra, yellow chakra
Number	Three, the third chakra
Location	Upper stomach, between your tummy button and breastbone
Associations	Personal power, sense of purpose, the ego; setting goals and boundaries; psychic ability, gut intuition
Related organs	Upper digestive organs, including the stomach, liver, diaphragm, adrenal glands; the immune system
Sense	Sight
Element	Fire
Age	15–21 and 64–70
When in balance	Feeling energetic, confident and focused; can stand up for yourself, get things done, trust your gut intuition
When weak or damaged	Struggle to make decisions; lack of direction; passive and submissive; afraid to challenge yourself; physical problems including stomach pains or low energy; inability to digest things
When over-developed	Workaholic; driven, obsessive and a perfectionist; angry, anxious and reactive; addiction
Symbol/yantra	A ten-petalled lotus; the triangle in the middle represents fire
Phrases	I do, I act, I am powerful, I am energetic, I can
Crystals	Try yellow crystals, such as citrine, to boost energy, focus the mind and set boundaries

I love
sunshine

I've got a
good gut
instinct

I had fun
during my
adolescence and
student days
(aged 15–21)

I know what
I want to do
in life

I love
watching
a real fire

I react
quickly

I can say
"No" when
I need to

Success is
important to
me, and I'm
not frightened
of it

My upper
digestion,
particularly my
stomach, works
pretty well

When I've got a
project, I like to
drive it forward
and get it finished

If I deserve
it, I can ask
for more
money

I prefer
to be
in control

I am a
confident
person

I know
where I am
going and I
don't let other
people knock me
off course

I like to
be busy

I am Powerful

The yellow solar plexus chakra is linked with energy, WILL POWER and the element of FIRE.

Its Sanskrit name is Manipura, which, rather exotically, means lustrous gem. When it's working well, it gives you the glowing jewels of power, vitality, SELF-CONFIDENCE and transformation.

You could think of it as your own personal power pack – the rocket booster that helps you move forward, to ACHIEVE whatever you set out to do. Solar plexus energy is much more focused than sacral chakra energy.

A healthy solar plexus chakra is linked to a HEALTHY EGO. When it is working well, you know what you want to ACCOMPLISH – and you go for it. It helps you to set boundaries, and stops you getting tangled up in other people's problems. If you want to have an open, generous heart chakra you need a strong solar plexus to support it, so that you don't become drained (for more on this, see page 83). This chakra is strongly linked to the ages of 15–21, when teenagers experiment with their identity and move toward independent adult life.

It is named after the spaghetti junction of nerves known as the solar plexus (solar because they radiate out like the sun's rays), located between your navel and breastbone. This area also includes the stomach, liver and adrenal glands. Like all the middle chakras, it projects both forward and backward.

This area is also in charge of your GUT INTUITION. It can tell you immediately if you've met the person you are going to marry, or if you've walked into the house you are going to buy. It might feel like excitement, certainty or forward motion in the pit of your stomach. This kind of major choice often feels surprisingly easy and healthy, when your brain has nothing to do with the decision-making process.

Conversely, if you feel a deep dread in your solar plexus, it can be a warning to change direction immediately. This is an ANCIENT SURVIVAL MECHANISM, when your body needs to warn you that something is dangerous or untrustworthy. This gut intuition rooted in your physical body feels very different from the cerebral higher intuition of your third eye.

When the
Solar Plexus Chakra is Balanced

When your solar plexus is working well, you have lots of ENERGY. You can get a great deal done and it doesn't feel like too much of an effort. You understand the principle that if you keep heading in the right direction, you will end up where you want to be.

Even though you have the same amount of time as everyone else, you have the mysterious knack of using it well. You are ORGANIZED and FOCUSED, and while other people talk about going to the gym, learning the guitar or booking tickets for a date night, you simply get on and do it.

You have tremendous DRIVE and ENTHUSIASM and inspire other people with your positive attitude. You may have natural authority within your family or be a good boss at work. If you believe in what you do, you are also a dream employee, because you take the initiative, work hard and can be relied upon to do a good job, without anyone nagging you.

If you encounter problems, you set out to work your way around them. A keyword for this chakra is TRANSFORMATION. You know that, with focused energy, almost anything – including yourself – can be transformed, improved or healed. This core belief gives you a quiet SELF-CONFIDENCE and a POSITIVE OUTLOOK. Because you look for solutions, or stepping stones toward your goals, you tend to find them.

This chakra is located in your stomach, but is also linked to a clear brain and EMOTIONAL INTELLIGENCE. You can make decisions easily and don't get bogged down by conflict or clingy people. You can stand your ground, find it easy to say "No" and, if something is unacceptable, you can use your anger constructively to create change.

When the solar plexus chakra is in balance you can feel like Superman or Superwoman, but if it is underpowered or overpowered, you are more likely to feel like a drippy doormat or to flip into anxious workaholic mode.

Recognizing when the
Solar Plexus
Chakra is Weak or Damaged

When this chakra isn't charged up properly, you are like a torch with a flattish battery: you don't glow very brightly. EVERYTHING SEEMS TOO BIG, too overwhelming. It's an ordeal dragging yourself out of bed in the morning, HARD MAKING A DECISION about what to wear and a struggle to get out of the door on time.

You might have all sorts of plans to boost your energy, such as doing more exercise, eating better food or giving up cigarettes, but you suspect they're going to be hard work. You might also have good intentions about finding a more interesting job or starting your own business...but not just yet. Meanwhile that bucket list of all the things you've been meaning to do for ages – clear out your attic, learn to scuba dive or drive through Paris in a sports car with the warm wind in your hair – seems completely out of reach.

Part of the trouble could be that other people take you or granted. And if you are LACKING DIRECTION, you may find yourself drawn to bosses or partners who have very strong solar plexus chakras and big egos,

and who sweep you along in the current of their own life. Alternatively, you might bury yourself in a job where you don't need to take any initiative, putting up with MUNDANE WORK in an organization with a rigid hierarchy. The idea of being able to step out of the cage, and think for yourself, might even panic you.

In the worst situations you may allow yourself to become the VICTIM in an abusive, dysfunctional relationship, at home or at work. Even if things aren't that bad, you may still think of yourself as the victim rather than standing your ground or walking out.

The reasons for a weak solar plexus chakra include very controlling parents or teachers, which meant you never learned the skills to motivate yourself or stand up for yourself as a teenager. Failing exams at school, a business collapse or a terrible accident (especially if you were at fault) can make you lose confidence in yourself and NOT WANT TO TRY again. Being bullied at school or work, or being badly treated by your partner, can also make the solar plexus shrivel up energetically.

Recognizing when the
Solar Plexus
Chakra is Over-developed

Most often this chakra becomes over-developed to cope with the fast pace of modern life, where we find ourselves running faster and faster simply to stand still – like a hamster trapped on a wheel. You achieve a lot, but don't have time to enjoy the fruits of your hard work, as the desire to achieve more pushes you forward to the next project. You find it HARD TO SWITCH OFF and might suffer from insomnia.

You may or may not be competitive with other people, but you are certainly COMPETITIVE WITH YOURSELF – even a perfectionist. You set high standards: to move faster, earn more, do everything better.

Though you can keep other people's demands at bay, you may struggle to say "No" to yourself. You might overachieve on your fitness targets, or feel compelled to keep up with your social media: keeping your body and brain busy all the time. You can be fiery, nervy and IRRITABLE; if your adrenal glands are overworked you may even burn up.

ADDICTION is particularly relevant for this chakra. What might start as a sacral chakra impulse (pleasure from smoking a cigarette, say, or playing a round of Candy Crush) can become a solar plexus impulse – a driving force over which you have no control.

If this chakra is really dominant, you can become thick-skinned and EGOTISTICAL. What you want to do takes priority, and it's irritating if other people get in the way. In extreme cases you might even become A BULLY, brow-beating everyone around you, in order to come first and make yourself feel more powerful.

WHAT HAPPENS TO OVERALL FLOW IF THE SOLAR PLEXUS CHAKRA ISN'T BALANCED?

If this chakra is underpowered, ideas flowing downward from our higher self get stuck, for there is no willpower to make them happen.

If the chakra is overpowered, it is hard for energy to flow upward. We can get stuck striving to become important in the world, or fritter away our talents in busy work, running around doing a lot, but not achieving anything that is really meaningful to us.

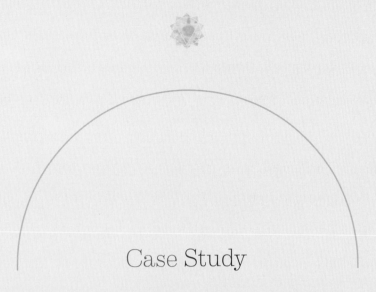

Case Study

WHEN THE SOLAR PLEXUS CHAKRA IS WEAK

Olivia had a steady job. She didn't really enjoy it, but didn't make any moves to find another one. She wanted to find a boyfriend, but didn't like the sound of using a dating app, and was too tired to go out to meet any men. She wanted to give up smoking, but hadn't got round to that, either.

She didn't really have the motivation to change her life at all, until her younger brother moved into her flat. He was so clinically depressed that he drained every last drop of Olivia's energy. Olivia didn't realize how ill and tired this made her feel, until she went on holiday. Away from her brother, she felt alive for the first time in months. She realized that she wanted to apply for a job abroad, but felt she couldn't leave her brother behind.

In treating Olivia, I had to clear off layers and layers of energy from her body, before I could feel any energy at all in her solar plexus chakra. First we cleared her brother's depression, which hung like a black cloud around all her chakras. Then a tight layer of family guilt, which clung like a wetsuit to her body. Underneath this her solar plexus had a beautiful bright yellow glow, but it was faint.

We looked at ways to boost her energy. Reluctantly Olivia admitted that she would like to give up coffee and chocolate as well as cigarettes. She agreed to start small, by drinking one extra glass of water a day when she had her first morning coffee, and walking for five minutes while she had her first lunchtime cigarette. This way, she had more chance of making permanent changes, as her body wouldn't be trying to sabotage her.

We cleared two past lives. In the first, Olivia's spirit had been an old lady who had tried to escape an earthquake but got trapped under rocks and died. Her dying thoughts were: "I shouldn't have moved. I should have stayed where I was." In the second, her spirit was a young man who acted hastily, got into a fight and was stabbed to death. Olivia had a deep sense that the man who stabbed him was reincarnated as her brother. She began to understand why she felt such visceral fear at the thought of confronting him – and of taking action in general.

After our session, Olivia told her parents that she couldn't look after her brother forever before telling him that she was planning to move abroad. She is looking for jobs and, to boost her CV, is volunteering at an environmental charity, where she has met some like-minded souls, both male and female.

How to Heal the
Solar Plexus Chakra

Working with the solar plexus chakra can give you back your spark and reboot your energy.

If you are already feeling anxious that this is going to be difficult, remind yourself that you don't need to do it all. Take things slowly and pick out just one or two ideas to bring some fire and passion back into this area.

If you suspect that your solar plexus is already spinning too fast, there are also some suggestions to soothe it and slow it down.

Focus on
YELLOW

The solar plexus chakra is linked to the colour yellow. Each time you notice something from the yellow spectrum, it's a reminder to focus on it.

Look out for lemons, sunflowers and daffodils, bales of straw and hay, mustard on your plate, a new pencil, candle flames, sand on the beach, pictures of lions and antelopes, the clasp of your watch strap or the glint on a gold wedding ring. If it's sunny, notice how the sunlight makes everything else glow.

Wear something yellow, even if it is small, such as a T-shirt with a flash of yellow (double points if the yellow part is over your tummy). You could also light a candle (to remind you of the link with the element of fire) or put some yellow flowers by your computer (to remind you of being productive).

While you are working on this chakra, you could gather items for a little altar, or post pictures of yellow items on social media, to focus your intention.

Feed your
Solar Plexus Chakra

According to studies, yellow food is the colour most likely to make us feel happy, perhaps because we associate it with sunshine.

Look out for yellow fruit: bananas, lemons, grapefruit, pineapples and star fruit, also golden varieties of apples, pears, plums, peaches, nectarines and melons.

Yellow vegetables include sweetcorn, peppers, squash and edible yellow courgette flowers. There also are loads of vegetables that come in unusual golden varieties, including yellow tomatoes, courgettes, beans, potatoes, beetroot, turnips, edible mushrooms and extraordinary Day-Glo yellow cauliflower. Yellow spices include saffron and golden turmeric.

Almost any egg, cheese or corn dish is likely to be yellow, including scrambled eggs, omelets, custard, macaroni cheese, polenta, corn grits and anything else with a golden crust.

When you eat these foods, set the intention to use their wonderful, optimistic colour to strengthen your yellow chakra. If your stomach is feeling anxious or stressed, take a couple of breaths before you start, and try to eat your food slowly, chewing every mouthful well.

Heal your
Physical
Body

If you want to feel more energetic and powerful, start with your physical body.

CHANGE YOUR POSTURE

People with self-confidence tend to stand up straight. People who can't stand up for themselves literally can't do this; they buckle in the middle. And people who throw their weight around often stand with their chest and stomach jutting out.

Feel weak or overwhelmed? Try standing up straight, in a power pose like Wonder Woman, with your feet firmly on the ground, head up, shoulder blades pulled down and hands on your hips. According to Harvard psychologist Amy Cuddy, the author of *Presence*, even two minutes in this pose can calm down your stress hormones, boost your testosterone and make you more likely to be hired for a job. For extra cheerfulness, look upward for a few seconds and smile. If your abdominal muscles are weak, try signing up for Pilates or yoga or doing some good old-fashioned sit-ups.

DETOX YOUR DIET

Suspect that your stomach and liver could do with a bit of a detox? Eat more soup, salads or vegetable smoothies, and cut back on alcohol and fat.

JUST DO IT

If you find that you are resistant to the idea of exercise, don't worry, just start small. Gather enough oomph to put on your trainers and get out of the door. You might just find that you carry on walking.

Exercise can make you feel less anxious by calming down the stress hormones, and can shake off the frowsty feeling that you can get from procrastination. If you manage to get some aerobic exercise, you may even feel a rush of mood-boosting endorphins.

FIRE BREATHING

The breath of fire, or Kapalabhati, is a form of rhythmic yoga breathing, using your stomach muscles to expel air through your nose. It stimulates the solar plexus to generate heat, massages your digestive system and helps you regain control when you are feeling stressed.

1 Sit comfortably and take a deep breath IN through your nose.

2 Quickly draw in your upper stomach toward your spine. This stimulates the diaphragm muscle so that you exhale fast, in a snort, through your nose.

3 Let your stomach relax and the air will flow into your lungs again naturally.

4 Keep pulling your stomach in and releasing it, until you have built up quite a fast rhythm.

Tune into your
Solar Plexus Chakra

The solar plexus chakra is connected to the element of fire. This section is about finding ways to think about power, stay calm and set good boundaries.

WORK WITH FIRE

The symbol of the solar plexus is a ten-petalled lotus, in the middle of which is an upside-down triangle representing fire. Every time you light a match or a candle it's a reminder that you are working on this chakra, and also of its power. One of the simplest ways to balance and heal this chakra is to gaze into a fire.

The fire that affects us every day is, of course, the sun. We should get 90 percent of our vitamin D from sunshine on our skin. If you are feeling unmotivated and lethargic, try spending more time outside, turning your face up to the sun; and perhaps get your vitamin D levels checked.

THINK POWER

Close your eyes and ask yourself who represents genuine power to you. (If your brain comes up with someone unpleasant, such as a psycho boss, rephrase the question: who represents the kind of power that you would like to have?) You might be surprised by the person who appears to you. They are almost certainly a clue as to how you would like to make your own mark on the world.

STAY CALM

Try walking away and breathing the next time you feel your stomach tightening with stress.

PROTECT YOUR FIRE

If any of your chakras are stuck wide open, or you work in an emotionally fraught place like a busy office or a hospital, you can feel ill or exhausted. A very good way to protect yourself is by putting energetic shields around your body. All of your chakras can benefit from some form of psychic protection, the heart in particular, but the focused, fiery solar plexus is the one to make this happen.

By concentrating on this chakra you can create healthy boundaries, look after your own energy and achieve what you set out to do. The more that is going on around you, the more important this protection is.

If any of your chakras are closed, and not enough energy is going through them, protecting your fire can also give them courage. When they feel safe, sensitive chakras like your throat often feel braver about opening up and expressing themselves.

One of my healing clients who works in a busy hospital, almost resigned because she felt so shattered every day. Everything changed when she started doing psychic protection exercises every morning on the train into work. I feel that if it works for her, in the acute ward of Accident and Emergency, it can work for anyone.

Here are some simple techniques:

o Send down energetic roots from your base chakra and feet (*see* page 44).

o Imagine drawing all your energy in round your body like a second skin (it can also help to imagine tucking it around you like a blanket). This centres your energy field and literally makes you feel less scattered.

o Imagine bringing yellow solar plexus chakra energy into your stomach, from the front and from the back. Visualize both streams coming together in a glowing ball of yellow energy just beneath your rib cage. Ask this wonderful, strong, fiery energy to carry the intention to protect you all through the day.

o With this aim in mind, close each one of your other chakras starting at the top. Imagine closing the petals of each chakra, like a flower that closes its petals at the end of the day. Or imagine shutting a little coloured door in front of each chakra. Choose whichever image works best for you.

o Imagine putting a protective crystal in front of each chakra, front and back. Either yellow to represent fire, or black tourmaline if you need something more solid. You could do this in real life, too (for more on crystals *see* page 172).

o Imagine that you are pulling a beautiful protective bubble of golden energy down over your head. Personally, I don't want to block all outside energy, I feel that this would make my life too dull. So I ask for the bubble to be high-tech and semi-permeable, so that everything I want and need for normal life can come through, including opportunities, inspiring ideas and a good connection between me and the people I love. That said, you can ask for the bubble to become tough like bulletproof glass when unpleasant or random energy comes along. Particularly if it isn't your responsibility. The more you practise, the easier this gets.

o If someone unexpectedly sends a nasty look, or a barbed comment your way, you can also put on emergency armour. Imagine quickly pulling down a screen of fiery, gold energy in front of your body, with an extra mirror over your heart (or over the earpiece of your phone) so that the unpleasant energy bounces back towards them.

o If you start to feel drained in a crowded place, or you are having a tough day, repeat the whole exercise several times. When you get home, you can also clean up your energy field by imagining a shower of light. For more on this *see* page 171.

Solar Plexus Chakra Meditation

HOW TO DO DIFFICULT THINGS

If you ask someone with a healthy solar plexus how they power through difficult or mundane jobs, they might look surprised and say something annoying like "I haven't thought about it. I just get on with it."

You may have many areas of your life that you can also "just get on with", without problems. But if you have projects that seem difficult, dull or make you anxious, try some energy work to power up your solar plexus chakra.

○ Close your eyes, and imagine a beautiful golden ball of light in your upper stomach, like gentle golden sunshine. Take long, slow breaths, basking in this light until it calms you.

○ When you feel relaxed, you can turn up the intensity. Imagine that the light gets brighter and stronger, like the sun itself. You might even find that it transforms into a beautiful fiery flame. Imagine the light or the fire as a feeling of excitement and confidence in your tummy. Allow the colour and the feeling to flow down into your body, so that you get a tingle of excitement in your fingers and toes.

○ If you feel resistance in any part of your body, ask the light to dissolve it, or the flame to burn it away.

○ Then, with all that strength and power inside you, imagine yourself doing the task, breezing through it. Imagine your arms, legs, eyes and hands, full of confidence; see and feel exactly what they do.

○ Lastly, visualize yourself looking happy and confident with the task already done. You might see the report written and printed, or you standing in the gym, smiling after a tough workout.

○ You can adapt this solar plexus exercise for almost any situation, and if you do it several times, to make it vivid, you might be amazed how effective it can be.

Heart
Chakra

Ancient Sanskrit name	Anahata (meaning: unstruck)
Commonly known as	Heart chakra, green chakra
Number	Four, the fourth chakra
Location	Middle of the chest, in the area of your physical heart
Associations	Unconditional love, compassion, healing; healthy detachment; balance
Related organs	Heart, lungs, upper back, shoulder blades, arms and hands
Sense	Touch
Element	Air
Age	22–28 and 71–77
When in balance	Benevolent view of the world, thinking well of other people; kindness to yourself and others; ability to maintain emotional boundaries; being present
When weak or damaged	Difficulty in giving or receiving love; low self-esteem
When over-developed	Highly sensitive; burned out by giving away too much love and being drawn into other people's emotional dramas
Symbol/yantra	A 12-petalled lotus; the two interlocking triangles in the middle represent matter and spirit, and masculine and feminine
Phrases	I love, I am loved, I am loving
Crystals	Try green or pink crystals, such as green aventurine and rose quartz, to nourish self-love, boost your capacity to heal others and stay balanced

I am emotionally sensitive

It's easy to see another person's side of the story

I like to help other people, particularly if they have problems

I am welcoming

I am open-hearted

I feel loved

I feel responsible for other people and how they feel

I sometimes shed a tear in sad movies (and happy ones)

I find it hard to say "No"

I enjoy my own company

I am empathetic – other people's happiness and pain affect me

Unkind words can affect me strongly

I'd do anything for my friends

I can tell my partner, family and friends that I love them

I'm a good person – I'm okay

I am Loving

The beautiful heart chakra represents unconditional love, healing and a benevolent connection with the world.

As you move through the rainbow colours of the seven chakras, the green heart chakra represents the midpoint between earth and heaven, connecting the three earthly lower chakras to the three ethereal higher chakras above. It is the centre of the rainbow bridge, the balance point between matter and spirit, earth and heaven.

It has two equally important aspects: the ability TO LOVE and TO BE LOVED. Because a healthy heart chakra can receive as much energy as it transmits. This is not just about loving and nurturing your partner, your friends and your children; it is also about allowing them to love and cherish you.

Part of the process of unfolding the heart chakra is about liking and loving yourself; if this idea seems weird or makes you feel uncomfortable, think of it as treating yourself with the KINDNESS and RESPECT that you would extend to anyone you care about.

While the solar plexus chakra is about establishing our sense of self, the heart chakra is about beginning to realize that we are all CONNECTED together. Part of the spiritual journey upward through the chakras consists of noticing the divine spark in everyone and everything (including the earth). We might get glimpses of this in every chakra, particularly the crown chakra, but when we feel this connection in our heart centre it is COMFORTING – like being suspended in a warm soup of loving energy. By consciously tuning into this loving energy in the universe, we can HEAL others and let it heal us.

The heart chakra is located in the middle of the chest. As well as governing the physical heart, it also governs the lungs, middle back, shoulder blades, arms and hands. It is associated with the ages of 22–28. But in my experience, once we get into the higher chakras, the age-band becomes less important.

When the
Heart
Chakra is Balanced

When your heart chakra is working well, you are a pleasure to have around. You are warm, POSITIVE and assume the best about other people. Like a really friendly dog, you don't mind showing how PLEASED you are to see the people you like and love.

Because you are OPEN-HEARTED you can express your feelings, and you are NONJUDGMENTAL when other people reveal theirs. You don't play mind games, and you can move beyond surface chit-chat quite easily, to create strong, intimate relationships.

You are BALANCED and emotionally intelligent. So if other people behave badly or speak sharply, you tend not to take it too personally or allow it to press your buttons. You are COMPASSIONATE and enjoy helping others, but can remain detached enough not to be manipulated or sucked into a drama.

You may be drawn to CARE for people, either consciously as a nurse or healer or semiconsciously as the mother hen or father figure in the office. But this works on a deeper level, too. When your heart chakra is well balanced, you don't actually have to do or say anything at all; other people feel better simply when you are around.

Physically, your heart and lungs are STRONG, your posture is upright and your shoulders are quite FLEXIBLE. This chakra is linked to the element of air. When it is working well, the energy flows through the heart chakra, like air flowing evenly in and out of a healthy set of lungs.

But when the heart chakra is out of balance, it's another story. This chakra can be underpowered, overpowered or even a mixture of both.

Recognizing when the
Heart
Chakra is Weak or Damaged

When your heart chakra isn't spinning properly, it is hard for energy to come in or out. You might have LOW SELF-ESTEEM and feel that you are UNWORTHY OF BEING LOVED. When compliments, warmth and love come your way, you might not even notice them, or you might shrink away.

If your heart chakra is very closed, you may come across as unresponsive or STONY-HEARTED. When too much emotion flies around, you may retreat because it feels uncomfortable, relying instead on gut instinct or your cool, logical brain. You might not see the point of a tender, loving heart chakra, but without it, your behaviour can be puzzling or even HURTFUL, and you have less chance of developing fulfilling relationships.

If your heart has been badly damaged in the past, by difficult parents, school bullies, the end of a relationship or a bereavement, you can FEEL BRUISED and broken-hearted and it really does hurt. Like scar tissue on a wound, your heart chakra temporarily or permanently closes up, so that you don't have to experience any more pain.

When my healing clients have been bereaved, they usually have a large energetic barricade over their heart area, which won't allow my hands to come too close. I always respect this, because often the heart needs to be left alone for a while to heal. It may take months or years, but even a traumatized heart chakra can open again, so that they can love – and be loved – again.

Recognizing when the
Heart
Chakra is Over-developed

When the heart chakra is spinning too fast or stuck wide open, you are at the mercy of other people's emotions.

You may be HIGHLY SENSITIVE and may feel it physically in your own body, when anyone around you is unhappy or in pain. Like a satellite dish, your heart picks up on so many emotional frequencies that you may feel EXHAUSTED by big family gatherings or busy places, such as airports and supermarkets.

As the old adage goes, people are either radiators or drains. The first type beams out good energy, while the second type sucks the life force out of you. If your heart chakra is wide open, you need to be wary of the energy vampires who will take advantage of your good nature.

It is easy for you to get sucked into EMOTIONAL DRAMA, and you are a soft touch for any kind of sob story. When you feel other people's pain so strongly, you may move heaven and earth to help them feel better, whether or not they have asked you to help. You may know, deep down, that other people's problems are not your responsibility and that they need these emotional lessons to help them grow, but that doesn't stop you piling in to fix or rescue them.

Alternatively, you may be extremely DRAMATIC AND NEEDY, pouring your heart out inappropriately and sucking in other people's time and energy.

WHAT HAPPENS TO OVERALL FLOW IF THE HEART CHAKRA ISN'T BALANCED?

As the centre of rainbow bridge, the heart chakra should be the point of balance, stillness, peace and calm.

If it is out of balance, it is difficult for the energy to flow either upward or downward, and your earthly and spiritual sides may have a hard job integrating.

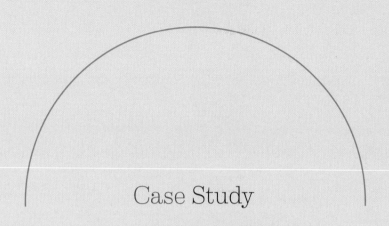

Case Study

WHEN THE HEART CHAKRA IS TOO OPEN

Alice is one of the kindest people I have ever met. Her biggest pleasure in life is to make other people happy, and she almost never stops smiling. Mysteriously, Alice married someone who was mean, grumpy and rude. The tetchier he became, the harder she tried to make him happy. Her boss was also surly and unpleasant, but Alice stayed looking after everyone in the office for years, keeping the atmosphere as happy as it could be.

She booked a healing appointment because she often had an upset stomach, which she suspected might be irritable bowel syndrome. Her heart chakra was absolutely wide open and shining like a searchlight. But in her sacral chakra I was given the image of a warehouse man, deluged with parcels. This chakra wanted to tell her it was sick

of the heart chakra being so generous and taking on so much, then dumping other people's problems down in her belly. I asked Alice to imagine opening up some of the parcels and, to her surprise, they were full of brown slurry. She began to understand that she was taking on everyone else's muck, but couldn't process it.

Alice didn't want to stop being kind. It made her happy and gave her energy, but we worked to connect the heart with the solar plexus, to set better emotional boundaries, and particularly to keep out people who didn't want or deserve her help. She agreed to do some psychic protection and to clear herself energetically at the end of the day (for more on this, *see* pages 83 and 171).

How to Heal the
Heart Chakra

The balancing exercises for this chakra are less practical than for the lower chakras, but are even more about energy and intention.

You may want to concentrate on suggestions to open up your heart chakra – to feel life fully, and to give and receive more love. Or focus on suggestions to help others without depleting your own energy.

Pick out a few points that feel right to you, and see where they take you. If you enjoy them, you might also like to try a healing workshop or Reiki course.

Normal life will also send you plenty of ways to stretch and heal your heart chakra.

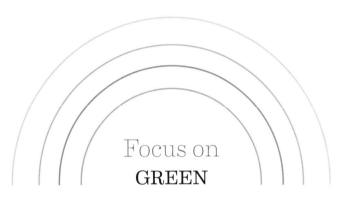

Focus on
GREEN

The heart chakra is linked to the colour green: a bright, grass green. Look out for other greens across the spectrum, from the pale, fresh green of new leaves, to the deep, dark green in the depths of a forest.

If you live in the country there may be green all around you, but even if you live in the city, you might be surprised by how much of this colour you see.

Unusually, this chakra is also associated with pale pink. Pink doesn't fit into the rainbow spectrum, but it is such a soothing heart-centred colour that it's good to add a dash of it occasionally.

See how many green things you can spot: a cat with gooseberry-green eyes, khaki-coloured rubber boots, jade earrings or a racing-green car.

Wear something green (double points if the green is over your chest) – or put a green leafy plant somewhere in the heart of your home.

You could make a little altar, perhaps with green flowers or heart-shaped objects, or post pictures on social meadia. As usual, this is about focusing your intention.

Feed your
Base Chakra

There is an abundance of green food, and as most of it is full of chlorophyll, it is very good for you. Look out for green vegetables and salad ingredients, including lettuce, avocado, celery and cucumber; the cabbage family, including kale and broccoli, plus all sorts of peas and beans, including edamame. You might also see courgettes, leeks, artichokes, asparagus, fennel, pak choi, okra and green varieties of tomatoes, peppers, squash, chilies and lentils.

Green fruit includes limes, kiwis, green varieties of apples, pears, plums, grapes, gooseberries and mangoes and, if you are feeling brave, wheatgrass juice. For pink, add dragon fruit if you can find it, or a lovely watermelon.

There are also masses of herbs, seeds and nuts to add a dash of green to all your food – including fresh parsley, chives and basil, plus pistachios, pumpkin seeds and even seaweed.

When you eat this green (and occasionally pink) food, set the intention that you are using its healthy colour to heal your heart chakra.

As this chakra is connected with healing, you could also experiment with blessing your food. Studies show that when healers send energy and loving thoughts into water used to irrigate plants, the plants grow taller and more healthy than the control group. Try setting the intention to send good energy into your own food.

Heal your
Physical Body

● Reconnect with your heart and lungs: what do they need?

STAND UP TALL AND OPEN UP

Go to a physiotherapist to free up your chest area. Most of us spend far too much time in front of the computer or on mobile phones. It's ironic that even when we click "like, like, like" on Facebook or Instagram, or text smiley emojis to our friends (which should be good for the heart chakra), the repetitive movement freezes up the muscles in our back and shoulders.

DO SOME AEROBIC EXERCISE

Almost any exercise is good, and aerobic exercise is particularly beneficial for your heart and lungs. Exercising outdoors is better for you than going to a gym, and seeing green leaves and grass can further nourish your heart chakra.

HEALING BREATHING FOR YOURSELF AND OTHERS

Breathing can calm you down and focus your attention. If you add words and bring awareness to your heart, breathing can also become a very simple healing ritual. Here are three techniques for you to try. You can experiment with words that suit you.

1 BALANCE This brings healing energy into your body, and sends healing energy out into the world:

o As you breathe IN, think of the phrase "I breathe in harmony".

o As you breathe OUT, think of the phrase "I breathe out harmony".

o Repeat for several minutes.

2 HEALING YOURSELF This is an excellent technique if you are feeling upset, angry or lovelorn:

o As you breathe IN, think of the phrase "I breathe in goodness".

o As you breathe OUT, think of the phrase "I breathe out pain [or anger, or whatever word is appropriate]".

o Repeat for several minutes.

3 HEALING THE WORLD If you're ambitious, try this classic ritual used by Buddhist monks. It works by using your heart like a filter, so don't use it if you are already overloaded:

o As you breathe IN, think of the phrase "I breathe in disharmony".

o As you breathe OUT, think of the phrase "I breathe out love".

o Repeat for several minutes.

Tune into your
Heart
Chakra

The heart chakra is associated with the element of air. Every time you feel a breeze on your skin, the wind in your face, or breathe in clean air it is a reminder of this beautiful, light, airy chakra. This section is also about love, healing and feeling a connection to the world around you.

OPEN YOUR HEART CHAKRA

Here are some very simple, practical ways to open up your heart chakra:

o Smile.

o Say thank you.

o Give compliments. If you notice something you genuinely like, show your appreciation. (This is different from flattery, which is fake and has an ulterior motive.)

o Spend time with small children and cute animals; they are good at triggering oxytocin (known as the cuddle hormone).

o Spend time with open-hearted people, who see your good points and are comfortable in their own skin.

o Volunteer (I visit people in a retirement home in their 80s and 90s, and leave every week feeling happy and lucky to have spent time with them).

o Find something, or someone, to take care of – whether it is a pet, a plant or a person.

o Make firm plans to see the people you love.

o Watch romantic or family films with happy endings.

o Stroke a pet, book a massage, hold someone's hand, give and receive hugs, enjoy sex in a loving relationship – the heart chakra is also linked to the sense of touch.

SPEAK KINDLY TO YOURSELF

A healthy heart chakra is about being kind to yourself as well as others. Listen to the way you talk to yourself. If you use words and phrases that you wouldn't say to your worst enemy, then it is time to change them. If phrases pop up such as:

> "I'm fat / I'm useless / I'm a disaster / I totally messed up / I look hideous in that photograph / I'm not sporty / I'm not talented / I'm unlucky / I'm being stupid / I should be able to do this..."

notice them and resolve to say something much more sympathetic, as though you were being kind to a friend or reassuring a small child.

If you use that unpleasant, scornful voice to motivate you or to solve problems, you could also drop down into your solar plexus chakra and imagine a friendly, positive personal trainer, who can help you find more constructive ways to move forward.

BE GRATEFUL

A gratitude diary is one of the easiest ways to open up your heart chakra.

Start by noting down anything that you like or are grateful for – hot water, sunlight coming through green leaves, a smile from the supermarket checkout lady, the train arriving on time.

You could also note nice things about yourself (such as long eyelashes) or reasons that you are grateful to your body (legs that can walk, ears that enjoy music, and so on).

USE HEALING MANTRAS

Apparently, a Hawaiian psychologist called Dr Hew Len healed an entire hospital of mentally disturbed criminals without seeing any of them, using the traditional practice of reconciliation and forgiveness known as Ho'oponopono. He spent three years sitting in his office going through their notes, repeating four simple powerful phrases: "I love you. I'm sorry. Please forgive me. Thank you."

The idea was that he was taking responsibility for the shadow parts of himself, which were damaged, violent or unhappy – acknowledging them and letting them go. By healing himself, he was healing the same energy vibration in the hospital's patients.

I was sceptical about this, but tried out the technique and found it was so effective that I have taught it to other people. I found that it's particularly useful when you are affected by someone else's problems and they won't talk to you or seek help for themselves.

Try it if you have a close family member or friend who needs healing. It can also help if someone is being unpleasant to you, and you don't have the option of walking away; or if someone has hurt you, and you are still suffering because of it.

Sit or lie down for five minutes, somewhere safe and quiet.

Think of the person in question and repeat these phrases:

o   I love you.

o   I'm sorry.

o   Please forgive me.

o   Thank you.

Be aware of whatever comes up in your own body. You might be surprised by how powerful this practice can be and the way it can shift your relationships for the better.

Heart Chakra Meditation

THE HOTEL BELLHOP

What do you do if you are big-hearted and pick up other people's emotional baggage? Psychic protection can help (*see* page 83) but it is hard to be unaffected if you have small children, elderly parents, close friends or a partner who can all get upset and need your love.

It is likely that some of this energy – particularly from people you care about – will get in under the emotional radar. This is often fine, especially in loving relationships. But if your kind heart chakra can't cope and you are feeling anxious and tired, let me introduce you to the old-fashioned hotel bellhop.

You might have seen him in an old Hollywood movie or vintage Christmas advertisement: the smiling bellhop in his uniform and pillbox hat, arms piled high with suitcases and shopping. His job is to help people with their baggage, lighten their load and make the journey from the lobby to their destination easier.

The important thing about a professional bellhop is not only that he carries the baggage, but that he puts it down when he gets to the guest's room, so that his hands are free. It would be ridiculous if he carried the bags upstairs, then carried them down again, and kept hold of them all the way through the next few days. He wouldn't be doing his job properly, for either his old customers or his new ones.

If you are a heart-centred person and love helping other people, you need to be able to put emotional baggage down, too. There will almost certainly be more baggage coming your way soon, and even more in the days and weeks to come. If you wish to be ready to handle it, you need your hands free.

o With the thought of a bellhop in your mind, imagine your arms and hands piled high with suitcases and parcels. Visualize a heavy backpack on your back. If you think a lot about other people's problems, you might even be carrying another pile of parcels stacked on your head.

o Set the intention to put the cases and parcels down. Imagine placing the suitcases on the ground. With your hands free, you can lift the pile of parcels off your head and shrug off the heavy backpack.

o Flex your hands; roll your shoulders and neck.

o Take a deep breath.

o Feel how much freer your heart feels.

o Set the intention that you are happy to give temporary help, but not to carry other people's emotional baggage around forever. (For a further chakra cleanse, you can also try the shower one on page 171.)

Throat Chakra

Ancient Sanskrit name	Vishuddha (meaning: purification, clarity)
Commonly known as	Throat chakra, light blue chakra
Number	Five, the fifth chakra
Location	Front of the throat, back of the neck
Associations	Communication, speaking your truth, listening
Related organs	Neck, throat, shoulders, mouth, sinuses, ears
Sense	Hearing
Element	Ether
Age	29–35 and 78–84
When in balance	Ability to express yourself easily and effectively, without fear
When weak or damaged	Constrained voice; dislike confrontation; people talk over you; physical problems include sore throat, mouth ailments, blocked sinuses, stiff neck and shoulders, feeling like you have a lump in your throat
When over-developed	Overloud voice; never stop talking or interrupting; tendency to nag; people often try to ignore you
Symbol/yantra	A 16-petalled lotus; the circle within a triangle symbolizes the manifestation of sound
Phrases	I speak, I listen, I am truthful, I am authentic, I am expressive
Crystals	Try blue crystals, such as aquamarine, turquoise, aqua aura and blue tourmaline, to aid good communication

I can stand up for myself (I'd say I'm assertive, not aggressive)

I am comfortable chatting

I enjoy listening to other people

I notice when someone has a beautiful speaking or singing voice

I'm pretty straightforward and truthful

I can express my anger, in a constructive way

I don't usually offend people because I'm tactful, although I say what I mean

Communication is the key to good relationships

I've spoken in public (or I would like to, one day)

I like to pass on interesting things that I hear or read on social media

I enjoy writing and express myself well (even if it's only in texts or emails)

I can pour out my heart to the people I love, for I know they'll accept me

My opinion is as valid as anyone else's

Sometimes I love sitting in silence

Listening is as important as talking

I am Expressive

The sky-blue throat chakra is all about communication, words and sound. When this chakra is working well, you can SPEAK YOUR TRUTH and EXPRESS YOUR EMOTIONS freely. You are in HARMONY, with yourself and with the world. Speaking feels easy and comfortable, and so does singing (even if it's only in the bath).

The throat chakra is the first of the three upper chakras, and the energy around it feels quite fine and ETHEREAL. When the throat chakra is spinning properly, words flow out easily. You can speak and WRITE ELOQUENTLY, and you have no trouble speaking up at a meeting or in a crowd.

If what you say is what you truly feel, really believe and is in perfect alignment with the path you are meant to be on, then your words will be very powerful. Words from an evolved throat chakra are a UNIQUE EXPRESSION of who you really are. Even if you don't speak much and don't speak loudly, if you are speaking with INTEGRITY, then your words will resonate and you will be heard.

This chakra, located in your neck, points both forward and backward. It is the vital link between your head and your body. As well as the throat and voice box, it is linked to the mouth, sinuses, shoulders and thyroid. Importantly, it is also linked to the ears, so this chakra is also about LISTENING: to other people, to yourself, to your spirit and to the divine. When you can HEAR CLEARLY, you can trust your inner guidance; and when you listen to other people too, there is a good chance of genuine connection and communication.

When the
Throat
Chakra is Balanced

When your throat chakra is balanced, communication comes naturally to you. Your voice will probably sound pleasant and confident, without being strident. YOU CAN EXPRESS YOURSELF very clearly, without being pushy. You think before you speak, so you sound calm, with no disturbing undercurrents of emotion beneath the surface.

You might have a job where you speak in public, perhaps as a broadcaster or a teacher. You may also express yourself through music – either singing or playing an instrument. Or perhaps you write in some way for a living, although plenty of people with balanced throat chakras express themselves in other less obvious fields.

You understand yourself pretty well. YOU KNOW WHAT YOU NEED and you don't mind asking for it, although you express yourself in such a tactful, diplomatic way that other people are happy to listen to you and usually help you.

Best of all, you tend not to hide behind a protective mask. What you present to the world is pretty much who you really are inside. You may not be perfect, but YOU ARE AUTHENTIC and honest and therefore seem very trustworthy.

Recognizing when the
Throat Chakra is Weak or Damaged

When the throat chakra is blocked, it can be very hard to speak up for yourself. Speaking in public often comes up as people's worst fear (surprisingly, more scary than the fear of dying, which usually comes only second on the list). But you may find it difficult to express what you are thinking and feeling, even in normal life.

Perhaps your throat chakra has atrophied because you are exceptionally sensitive and DISLIKE CONFRONTATION. You might prefer to stay quiet so that you don't upset anyone or make them angry. You may find it hard to complain, or find yourself saying nothing, when you would rather say "No". Your voice might sound thin, weak or whispery, as though it lacks power.

But a weak or damaged throat chakra isn't just about difficulties in communicating with other people. It is also a symptom of NOT COMMUNICATING TRUTHFULLY with yourself. Instead of fully feeling and expressing your emotions, you may stuff them down. You may even feel this physically, as though you have a LUMP IN YOUR THROAT.

If you CAN'T EXPRESS YOUR NEEDS clearly, because you don't really understand how you feel, then you are unlikely to get much sympathy. If everything you say is slightly out of harmony with your true feelings, then your words will sound a bit off, and you may find that people ignore you or talk over you.

Recognizing when the
Throat
Chakra is Over-developed

It is a pleasure to spend time with someone who has a balanced throat chakra. But anyone with an overactive throat chakra can be a liability – the coworker with the foghorn voice who NEVER STOPS TALKING, the person at dinner who tells story after story but never asks a single question, or the lout in the quiet train carriage who shouts, "I'M ON MY MOBILE."

If your throat chakra is over-developed, you may love the sound of your own voice and even think of yourself as a good communicator. But if you never stop talking and INTERRUPTING or, worse, never stop NAGGING, other people might dread spending time with you. If your throat chakra isn't connected to your heart, then you might not realize, or care, how unbearable you may sound.

If you are lucky, your partner or friends will discreetly nudge you when you are talking or complaining too much, but if you don't change and you NEVER LISTEN, your relationships can run into trouble. You may find that the people you want to be close to, including your children, become selectively deaf – ignoring what you say, retreating behind noise-cancelling headphones or avoiding you altogether.

WHAT HAPPENS TO OVERALL FLOW IF THE THROAT CHAKRA ISN'T BALANCED?

If the throat chakra gets underpowered, you can feel disassociated from your body. It's a bit like damming up a river: you can think and think, but when the energy doesn't flow downward both your head and your body suffer, and the chakras can't support each other.

If your throat chakra is overpowered you can spend a lot of time and energy talking but not enough actually getting on with anything.

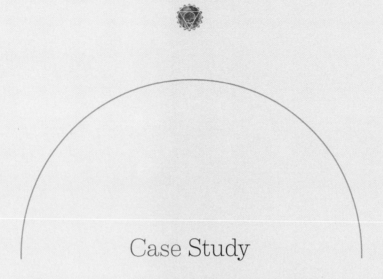

Case Study

WHEN THE THROAT CHAKRA IS TOO CLOSED

Sam was a delightful woman, with beautiful posture. She was a children's ballet teacher and said she had no trouble at work – her words flowed, and she could manage a class of a dozen children. But at home her husband and two daughters were often rude and disrespectful to her. She found it very hard to stand up to them, or to ask them for help around the house. She had a lot of sore throats, neck ache and, after a particularly big, one-sided argument with her daughter, in which she didn't speak up, she even got laryngitis and lost her voice completely for three days. After another one-sided argument with her husband, which hurt her feelings, she woke up two days running with blood in her mouth, from literally biting her tongue.

Sam's parents were both powerful characters who expected her to be obedient as a child, and her ballet teachers were even tougher, so she never really learned how to speak up as a child. But her fear of expressing herself seemed to run deeper than that.

During our work together, we found several past lives in which she had been hanged, decapitated and had her throat cut. When these had been cleared, we worked on strengthening her lower chakras to give her more courage. Then we connected them to her throat chakra to support anything she wanted to say. Sam says her neck feels more free now, and her family has started to be more respectful and supportive.

How to Heal the
Throat Chakra

Some of the best ways to unblock this chakra are by using your voice. But if you were shy, were criticized at school or were brought up in a children-should-be-seen-and-not-heard kind of way, you might be blanching at the thought of voice-work.

Don't worry, for there are other suggestions to try as well.

If you suspect that your throat chakra is already going faster than a runaway train (or your nearest and dearest are dropping heavy hints that you talk too much), then the listening exercises may be helpful. And to connect your throat to the other chakras, *see* page 170.

Focus on
BLUE

The throat chakra is linked to the colour blue, particularly a beautiful mid-blue, like the sea and the sky on a sunny day. Colour psychologists say that this tone is both uplifting and calming.

The colour blue has a particularly wide spectrum. As well as sky blue, you could look out for turquoise and aquamarine, right through to cobalt and navy blue.

The more you look out for this colour, the more you will spot it. See how many blue items you can pick out at home and out on the street: blue jeans, blue book covers, the lady on the train with peacock-blue hair.

Even if you live in a rainy climate, keep looking upward for blue sky and you will notice it more often than you did before. Turn your face upward and soak in the colour whenever you can. And wear something blue, perhaps starting with a blue scarf, tie or necklace (double points for anything around the throat).

You could make a little altar, with blue flowers and other blue objects, or post pictures of blue items on social media, to focus your intention on this chakra.

Feed your
Throat
Chakra

There's not much food that's naturally bright blue, apart from spirulina (a healthy natural food supplement made from blue-green algae), so you might have to be a bit more creative for this chakra.

You can add a beautiful flash of blue to salads, soups, puddings, drinks...almost any dish, by adding edible blue flowers such as borage, cornflowers, pansies, blue lavender and nigella (also known as love-in-a-mist).

You might also be able to find intriguing deep-blue potatoes and blue corn on the cob. The blue corn is most widely available as popping corn or blue corn chips.

You could also look out for darker blue food such as plums, damsons and blueberries, plus figs with a blue bloom.

All food, of any colour, usually looks great served on blue plates, and you could serve drinks in pale-blue glasses.

This chakra also benefits from liquid food such as soups and smoothies, and from delicious drinks including hot honey and lemon – anything that slips easily down your throat and feels soothing.

As the Sanskrit name for this chakra is Vishuddha, which means purification, focusing on this chakra could also be a good opportunity to cut down on processed food, or to give up alcohol or cigarettes.

Heal your
Physical Body

Looking after your head and shoulders is good for your throat chakra.

LISTEN UP

The throat chakra governs the neck, throat, shoulders, mouth, teeth, ears, sinuses, thyroid, parathyroid and the upper part of the oesophagus and trachea. This would be a good time to book a routine dental appointment, and to get your hearing tested.

LOOSEN UP

Of all the chakras, the throat benefits the most from regular physical movement. Your neck is carrying the equivalent of a large, heavy bowling ball around all day, often at a funny angle (have you ever watched someone texting and noticed how their head pokes uncomfortably forward?), so it's not surprising it gets tired and stiff. When your neck muscles tighten up, the energy flowing between your head and body – and through your throat chakra – can become blocked and sluggish..

o Gently move your head in a big circle: imagine that you have a pencil strapped to the top of your head and that you're drawing giant circles on the ceiling.

o Roll your shoulders forward and backward, and gently pull your shoulder blades downward – this takes a lot of pressure off your neck and instantly gives you better posture.

o Imagine a cord from the top of your head is pulling you upward, so that you stand taller and lengthen your neck.

If your neck still doesn't feel happy, call in the professionals: you might need a neck massage, Alexander Technique lessons or physiotherapy.

BLUE-WHALE BREATHING

If you ask a child to draw a whale, they would probably doodle a big body, a small tail and a big fountain of water coming out of the blowhole. Imagine the WHOOSH as the whale sends that water up into the air. This image can be really helpful in cleaning out any chakra, and is particularly good if you feel that your throat is blocked or underpowered.

1 Close your eyes and breathe IN. Focus on your throat. Imagine that you are gently breathing in through the middle of your throat chakra.

2 Hold the air in your lungs, then breathe OUT strongly, imagine the energy is whooshing out through a blowhole in your neck.

3 Repeat. Add the intention that each OUT breath is cleaning and clearing your throat chakra. (Bonus points if you make a little snorting sound through your nose.)

A variation of this is the Lion pose in yoga, where you breathe out strongly *and* stick out your tongue – another satisfying way to clean out the throat chakra.

Tune into your
Throat Chakra

The throat chakra is linked to the element of ether, a substance finer and lighter than air. This section will also focus on the power of words and ways that you can express yourself.

KNOW WHY KIND WORDS AND VIBRATIONS ARE SIGNIFICANT

Words and sounds have a very specific energy and vibratory pattern. Many religions believe that the universe was created with a word or primordial sound. But do words and vibrations have any effect on us?

The Japanese researcher Dr Masaru Emoto taped words such as "love" and "gratitude" onto containers of water, froze them and photographed the crystals. They were absolutely beautiful – as were the ice crystals that were exposed to music by Mozart and Vivaldi (*see* page 188 for details of his book).

But when he used words such as "fool" and "devil", or blasted the water with heavy-metal music, the crystals look dramatically and shockingly different: lumpy, asymmetrical, fragmented.

Can water be healed? Dr Emoto gave some water from a polluted water source to some monks to bless. They prayed and chanted over it. The crystals from the blessed water looked a lot better than those that remained unblessed.

What does it all mean? Human beings are 70 percent water, so our bodies are almost certainly affected by words and vibrations.

EXPRESS YOUR FEELINGS

Have you heard of the apple experiment? Put it to the test and see for yourself why expressing your feelings in words is important.

o Cut an ordinary apple in half, and put each half in a clear jam jar. Give one half a label marked "LOVE" and the other a label marked "HATE". Put them in different corners of the room.

o Say only nice things to the LOVE apple. Treat it like a favourite pet. Tell it how beautiful it looks; how much you love it; how you admire the colour of its shiny skin.

o Say only nasty things to the HATE apple. Behave like Cinderella's wicked stepmother. Tell it is a disgrace; that it is ugly and useless; that you despise it.

o Then see what happens.

A close friend tried this and the results were shocking. The LOVE apple looked wonderful for weeks. The HATE apple shrivelled up and went mouldy. This experiment seems to be good evidence that if you are angry or unhappy, it is important to express those feelings. Let them out of your throat chakra and inflict them on an apple, rather than letting them fester inside you. (*See* also the section on self-talk on page 103.)

SING

When I was working on my throat chakra, I signed up for singing lessons.

At the start of the first lesson, my heart was hammering. I had a lump in my throat and, when I opened my mouth, out came a wobbly little croak. But after a few minutes of laughing and breathing, I forgot my nerves. After a few weeks I was singing along to the piano, belting out songs from old musicals – sometimes tunefully. My confidence blossomed, and I am sure my throat chakra did, too. So why not try some of the following suggestions to boost your own throat chakra:

o Sign up for singing lessons, too: find a nice teacher, and choose songs you love.

o Join a choir; there are choirs for all levels of ability and experience.

o If nothing else, start singing when you are on your own. Sing along to the radio when you are stuck in traffic or doing chores (you might even enjoy yourself).

o Chant "OM". Even if you think you can't sing, you can definitely chant using one note only. You might already have tried it in a yoga class. Sit cross-legged and start a long "O" sound at your base chakra, allowing your attention to travel up your spine. When you get to your throat, close your lips and hum an "M" sound until you reach the top of your head. The vibrating sound you make in your throat is good for all your chakras. And you'll be helping to connect the flow of energy between your body, neck and head.

o Mantras can be very good for the throat chakra. Using a mantra is a form of meditation, where you repeat the same phrase, such as "Om mani padme hum", over and over again. You can sing, chant or say it. If your throat chakra is feeling too embarrassed to declare itself, you can repeat the mantra under your breath or in your head, because the rhythm and repetition are still beneficial for this chakra.

SPEAK UP

If someone is being a pain, they can literally give you a stiff neck, because they are stifling your throat chakra. It can be hard to speak up to a difficult parent, overbearing boss, grumpy flatmate or sassy teenager, but try the following exercise:

o Start by fixing an affirmation somewhere that you are likely to see it, such as on your bathroom mirror or refrigerator door. It could read, for example, "I am allowed to speak up" or "I can speak clearly" (if you live with mocking flatmates or sarcastic teenagers, you could shorten this to "TRUTH" or "CLARITY"; you will know what it means).

o Sit down and write the other person a letter. Don't hold back. Add some more. But – and this is important – burn the finished letter or tear it into tiny pieces and let it go. If you are still feeling upset or angry, punch a pillow, ideally when you are on your own and can give the pillow a good talking to. The idea is to get the hurt and fury out of your system. If you can get to a place of strength and calm, it will be much easier to have the conversation in real life.

o If this isn't enough, find a book or a course on assertiveness (being assertive doesn't mean being nasty or aggressive; it means speaking up in a polite, effective way). If you can't communicate with your partner, or you feel they don't listen to you, try an active listening course together. If your inability to speak up goes back to childhood, find a friendly inner-child therapist. With some of my healing clients we find that the block goes back even further, perhaps because they were born with a cord around their neck, or they had past lives where they couldn't speak up. When they've been released, they report back that the difficult people in their life seem less frightening. Some physical symptoms, such as neck aches, get better, too.

Throat Chakra Meditation

LISTEN TO YOURSELF

The throat chakra is linked to listening as well as speaking. And the most important person to listen to is, of course, yourself. We've all got so much wisdom tucked away, and if we calm down, we can start to allow it to flow up into our conscious mind.

The idea of silence can be quite a scary prospect. But be brave: try putting down your phone and taking yourself somewhere quiet. This doesn't have to be a week at a silent retreat: start with five minutes locked in the bathroom, or being on your own in the park at lunchtime.

You may find that your inner voice pipes up at this point, like an annoying, chattering monkey. It might ask you questions, nag you to do something more useful or tell you that you're not capable of sitting quietly (or, worse, that don't deserve to). How do you tame this monkey? For a few minutes, try focusing on just on the sound of your breath as it comes in and out of your body.

If your inner voice is really insistent, voicework teachers such as Hal and Sidra Stone suggest turning up the volume and really listening to what it has to say. Try writing down everything that comes up – however critical. When you really listen, in a benevolent, detached way, your negative inner voice eventually runs out of steam, and then you might find that a more beautiful, useful voice appears instead, with messages from your body, your guides or your soul.

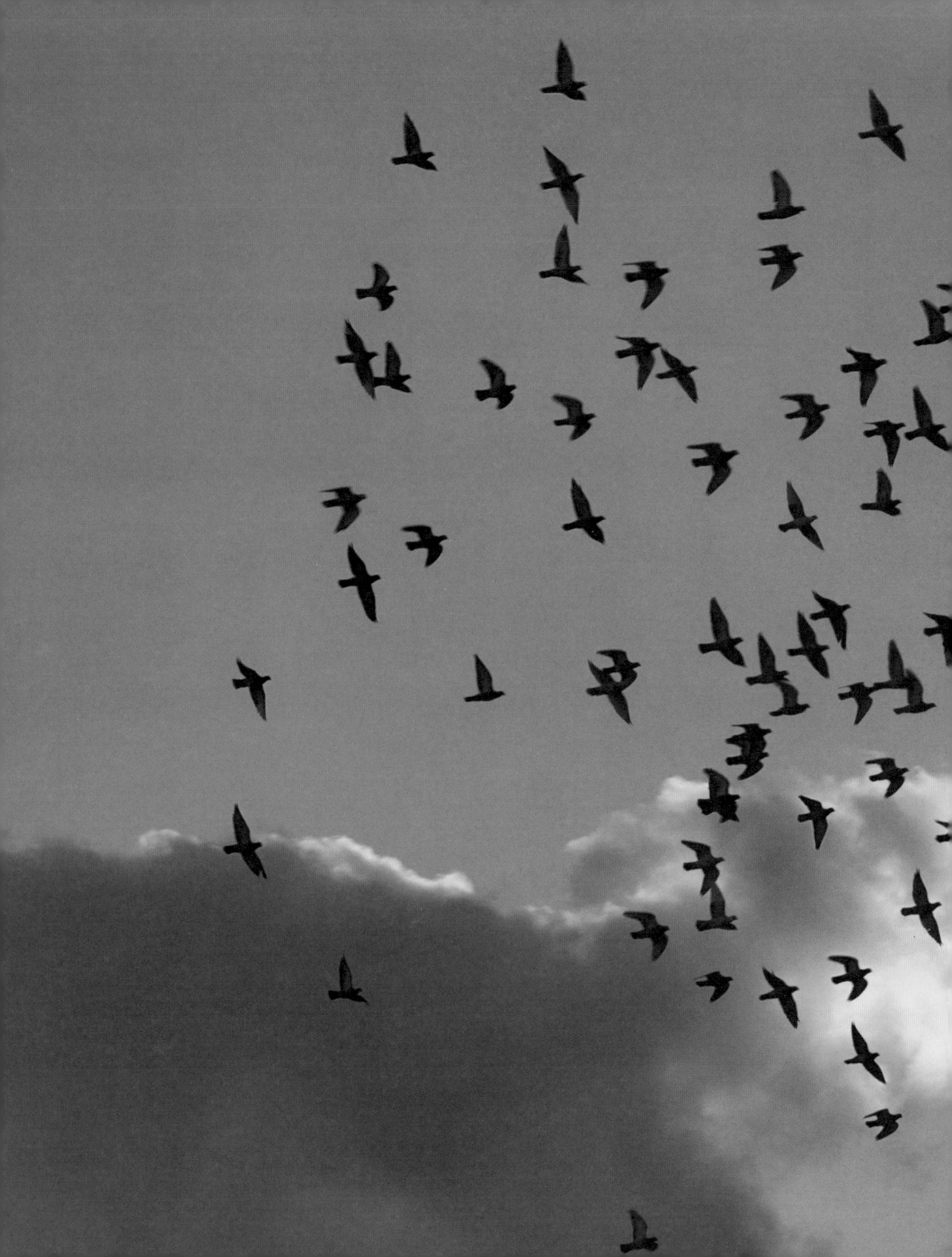

Third Eye Chakra

Ancient Sanskrit name	Ajna (meaning: to perceive, to command)
Commonly known as	Third eye chakra, brow chakra, indigo or purple chakra
Number	Six, the sixth chakra
Location	The brow, slightly above your eyebrows in the middle
Associations	Sixth sense, intuition, wisdom; spiritual awareness, seeing clearly; perspective, balance
Related organs	The eyes, brain, sinuses, pineal gland
Sense	Sixth sense or intuition
Element	Light
Age	36–42 and 85–91
When in balance	Clear brain, clear sight, imagination, insight; a balance between logic and intuition
When weak or damaged	Overly practical brain; struggle to be creative; narrow-minded and dismissive of others' opinions; detached from spirituality
When over-developed	Often feel overwhelmed or confused and struggle to concentrate or plan ahead; out of touch with reality; superstitious; suffer with feelings of delusion and paranoia
Symbol/yantra	A two-petalled lotus; the downward pointing triangle can represent wisdom
Phrases	I see, I understand, I am clear-sighted
Crystals	Try indigo or purple crystals, such as azurite and amethyst, to clear the brain and boost intuition

I am
a visual
person

I notice
beauty and
appreciate it

I have had psychic
experiences – such
as telepathy,
déjà vu or glimpses
of the future

Creativity and
logic are equally
important

I have
a good
imagination

I am sensitive
to atmospheres

I have seen,
heard or
sensed
spirits

I had imaginary
friends as a child;
sometimes I was
scared of the dark

Dreams are
fascinating

I know
the direction
I am going
in my life

I spend more time
up in my head
than in my body
– and I like it
that way

I find it
easy to
plan ahead

Sometimes
I take in so much
visual information
that it is
overwhelming

I think
a lot

I am
intuitive

I am Clear-sighted

If the journey upward through the chakras is like climbing a mountain, then you are now on the higher slopes and starting to get a good bird's eye view. The third eye chakra is located on the forehead, between and just above the eyebrows, where a Hindu lady might wear her red bindi.

In terms of your physical body, this chakra governs your two eyes and both hemispheres of the brain. So it is linked to CLEAR-SIGHTEDNESS and BALANCED THINKING.

On a spiritual level, it is in charge of your SIXTH SENSE, which can give you important insights and intriguing glimpses of the nonphysical world. The third eye is symbolic rather than scientific – an inner eye with PERCEPTION far beyond ordinary sight, and a doorway to the vivid limits of your IMAGINATION, memory or dreams.

In the lower chakras, psychic messages tend to show up physically as visceral gut feelings, whereas in the third eye chakra, psychic information usually comes straight into your mind, as a sort of KNOWING. When you think of somebody out of the blue just before they email you, this could be simply a coincidence. But if such coincidences happen a lot, it's your SIXTH SENSE working.

When the third eye is open, you might get messages via CLAIRVOYANCE (seeing with your inner eye), CLAIRAUDIENCE (hearing with your inner ear) or TELEPATHY. You might have glimpses of the future, be able to see ANGELS AND SPIRITS or communicate with your guides. Best of all, you may already be getting a sense that our physical reality isn't the only one, and that we are all parts of a GREATER REALITY.

But this chakra is also about equilibrium and staying in touch with reality. When it is working well, everything is paired up and nicely balanced. You can access both the LOGICAL AND INTUITIVE sides of your brain, take in a lot of information, but maintain perspective and see the big picture. You can view the physical outer world clearly, but can also trust your INNER WISDOM and messages from your spirit.

When the
Third Eye Chakra is Balanced

When this chakra is working well, you can see where you are going. It is like driving along with a sparkling clean windscreen in good weather, with the landscape spread out in front of you. On a human level, this may be because you have a clear brain and got yourself organized for the day. On a soul level, it's more profound; when your INNER VISION IS CLEAR, you know which direction you need to go in the long term so that your spirit can evolve.

The area around a healthy third eye chakra feels very clean. You don't let other people's priorities, emotions or general muddle cloud your own vision. If you do find yourself surrounded by other people's energy (the fog and squashed flies on your metaphorical windscreen), you will take steps to clear it away. (For more on psychic protection, *see* page 83.)

Because this chakra is so balanced, you use both the left and right sides of your brain. Your combination of logic and intuition means that YOU ARE WISE and can come up with PRACTICAL, CREATIVE solutions for all sorts of problems. You may read widely or take in information from many different sources, but you have the knack of simplifying everything and making it easy to understand. You can often see patterns, or an obvious path, when other people can't.

Visual beauty may be important to you, and you can appreciate details as well as the big picture. You may have a VIVID IMAGINATION and be able to conjure up images and stories with your words. You may be able to remember your dreams and get lots of information from them.

Your spirituality is important and you have a STRONG MORAL COMPASS. You have a sense that there is more than our physical reality, so you pay attention to your intuition and may be open to the idea of communicating with angels or spirit guides.

Recognizing when the
Third Eye
Chakra is Weak or Damaged

If your third eye doesn't open up properly, there won't be much information flowing in and out of it. This can make you NARROW-MINDED, and you will almost certainly miss out on some of the beauty of life.

In particular, if you block out anything that you can't actually see, touch, hear, taste or smell, you won't get the chance to appreciate the rich, colourful world of the spirit or the imagination. You might find it DIFFICULT TO VISUALIZE. Perhaps creative essays were hard and baffling for you at school and you still don't really see the point of reading fiction. You might not remember your dreams, or may shrug them off as unimportant. And you might dismiss intuition as a load of mumbo-jumbo.

If you insist that the only truths are logic and reason, you may cut yourself off from your spirituality. To you, life won't be a progression and an unfolding, but a workmanlike job that finishes when you die. If your lower chakras are strong, the markers of worldly success – such as getting a promotion or buying a better car – might be enough for you, but you may feel a slight EMPTINESS, a what's-the-point-of-it-all yearning that you can't quite put your finger on.

If you can't get perspective through this chakra, you might get bogged down by small details of human existence: drawn into petty squabbles or stymied by minor difficulties. If anyone has opinions or experiences different from your own (particularly when they talk about airy-fairy stuff such as angels), you may find it very uncomfortable and may squash them by being RUDE and DISMISSIVE.

If you were born into a logical, practical family, your sixth chakra may never have had the chance to open fully. Or you may have closed it down as a child, particularly if you were scared by ghosts, told off for making things up or bullied for being soft.

Recognizing when the
Third Eye
Chakra is Over-developed

When this chakra is stuck wide open, so much energy flows in and out that you can get OVERWHELMED, or LOSE TOUCH WITH REALITY.

This is partly a problem of modern life. If you live in a city, commute to work or use social media, you can be bombarded with images and information every day. Add in your own mental chatter, memories of the past and ANXIETIES ABOUT THE FUTURE, and you can be processing thousands of different thoughts. If you never take time out to rest your brain, it can be hard to know what is important.

If your third eye is also letting in too much psychic or subtle information, there's even more background noise. Some of these messages may be ambiguous anyway, and if you are overwhelmed, it can be hard to pick out an appropriate response. Instead you might JUMP TO CONCLUSIONS (my neighbour didn't smile at me this morning – I'm sure I've offended her) or become overly jumpy or SUPERSTITIOUS (I think I saw a magpie on the way to the airport, so should I cancel the flight?).

When the sixth chakra is spinning too fast, you might become ungrounded and spacey, suffer from brain fog or find it HARD TO CONCENTRATE, think clearly or plan ahead. Your imagination might run wild, to the point of DELUSION. You might even become paranoid and hallucinate. Personally I believe that ghosts are real, but if you see frightening ghosts and shadows that other very psychic people can't, then your third eye probably needs some help.

WHAT HAPPENS TO OVERALL FLOW IF THE THIRD EYE CHAKRA ISN'T BALANCED

If this chakra is underpowered, you can become narrow-minded. Like a blockage in a tube, it can be hard to progress upward if you don't believe in spiritual growth.

If the chakra is overpowered, you can become top-heavy and ungrounded. It is much easier to see clearly when you are properly rooted and can rely on physical sensations as well as your head.

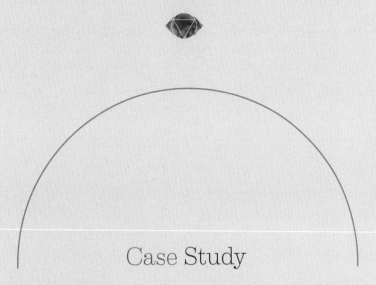

Case Study

WHEN THE THIRD EYE CHAKRA IS BLOCKED

John was a no-nonsense man who ran his own building business. When a property developer offered him a lucrative contract to refurbish some flats, he was delighted. But John's wife was uneasy. She had met the property developer and didn't like him. She kept saying (in a very annoying way) that John shouldn't go ahead. She couldn't give him any logical reasons, but begged him not to sign the contract until he had had time to think about it on holiday.

While they were in Spain, John got the news that the developer had been arrested and the property company was being investigated by the Serious Fraud Office. In the end the company went bankrupt, owing its workmen and suppliers crippling sums of money.

John admitted afterward that he had had doubts, too, but he had squashed them. Little clues about the developer's appearance and his behaviour made John's brain feel foggy and confused in their meetings, plus niggling doubts when he inspected the site only made sense afterward.

John had a serious crisis of confidence. How would he pick up the warning signals next time? He realized that his father had often used phrases such as "Don't be daft / Don't make a fuss about nothing / You don't know anything / Do as you're told", which he had internalized.

He is not going to start yoga or meditation classes any time soon, but his rigid attitude has softened, and he is now much better at trusting his wife's judgment – and paying attention to his own intuition when something doesn't seem quite right even if he can't explain why.

How to Heal the
Third Eye Chakra

Most of the suggestions that follow are about opening up your third eye chakra. If you suspect that yours is already too open, do some of the exercises from the lower chakras – particularly from the base chakra (*see* pages 40–43) – to get you grounded. You might also find helpful suggestions about psychic protection in the solar plexus chapter (*see* page 83).

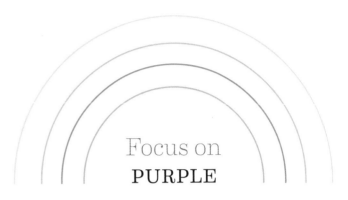

Focus on
PURPLE

Strictly speaking, if you stick to Newton's seven classic colours of the rainbow, the third eye chakra should be a dark bluish indigo. But as this shade has quite a limited range, it works just as well to associate this chakra with all sorts of beautiful shades of purple (leaving white and pale violet for the crown chakra).

So use your eyes to look out for purple everywhere – lavender, wisteria, jacaranda trees, a purple twilight, purple nail polish, a bishop's robes, distant purple mountains – and, each time you spot it, it's a reminder to focus on your third eye chakra. Also look out for light – light coming through something translucent and crystalline, such as an amethyst ring, can be doubly evocative.

Wear something purple or indigo: start with something small, such as purple-tinted sunglasses (double points for location near the eyebrows). Perhaps put a vase of purple flowers somewhere close to a window or a mirror, to remind you of inner vision.

You could make a little altar, or post pictures of purple items (and pictures relating to eyes) on social media.

Feed your
Third Eye Chakra

Purple food is often full of pigments known as anthocyanins, which are very good for you.

Look out for deep-purple vegetables, such as aubergines, cabbage and kohlrabi. Vegetables with a purplish tinge include purple-sprouting broccoli, onions, garlic, artichokes and asparagus.

There are also fabulously unusual purple varieties of carrots, peppers, radishes, potatoes, Swiss chard and surreal bright-purple cauliflower.

Indigo and purple fruits include blackberries, blueberries, blackcurrants, elderberries, figs, plums, black cherries and purple grapes.

You can also garnish your food with edible allium flowers (those wonderful purple balls of petals growing from onions, spring onions and chives) or use lavender and violet petals.

When eating purple food, set the intention that you are using its purple power to clarify your third-eye chakra.

You could also eat food that is good for the eyes and brain, including food containing beneficial fats, such as oily fish, avocado and walnuts, plus berries and multicoloured vegetables (if you have been working through the chakras, you've already got that covered).

Every time you make an effort to arrange your food attractively and stop to look at it before you eat, it's another reminder that you are focusing on this chakra.

Heal your
Physical Body

To balance your third eye chakra, look after your eyes, forehead and brain.

LOOK AFTER YOUR EYES

Do your eyes need testing? Could they do with a rest from the computer screen? (There are apps to remind you to look away every 30 minutes or so.) Most eyes benefit from spending time outside, where you relax your focus farther away.

Try rubbing your palms together to create heat, then holding your hands over your eyes for a few minutes. You could also seek out some eye exercises, to strengthen and relax them.

LOOK AFTER YOUR FOREHEAD

Book yourself in for a facial, head massage or some facial acupressure. If you can, book in for the Indian Ayurvedic therapy called Shirodhara, in which a stream of warm oil is dripped onto your forehead. It will certainly focus your attention on this area.

LOOK AFTER YOUR BRAIN

You could do fun puzzles to boost the left and right sides of your brain (the left brain is all about logic, order and detail, while the right brain is concerned with colour, intuition and creativity).

Meditation can clear and reboot your brain (*see* page 164 for more on meditation). Brain scans of Buddhist monks show that they have grown all sorts of extra neurons - the cells that transmit nerve impulses.

ADD IN SOME EXERCISE

British neurosurgeon Henry Marsh, who has seen the inside of many thousands of brains, looks after his own brain by running and cycling every day - including a sprint that leaves him breathless.

The rhythm of walking, swimming or riding can help your intuition to work well. As you move, you may find that answers pop up out of nowhere.

NOSTRIL BREATHING

This focuses your attention on each side of your face and is a good way to balance the left and right sides of your brain. It simply involves breathing through one nostril at a time.

1 Hold your left hand up to your nose.

2 Close your left nostril with your thumb. Breathe OUT and then IN, through your right nostril.

3 Release your left nostril then close your right nostril with your forefinger. Breathe OUT and then IN, through your left nostril.

4 Repeat on both sides, for several minutes, focusing on how the air feels on each side.

5 When you've got the knack of this technique, have another go, this time without your fingers, using intention.

Tune into your
Third Eye Chakra

The third eye chakra is linked to the element of light. This section is also about boosting your intuition, your vision and gaining perspective.

DEVELOP YOUR SIXTH SENSE

The third eye chakra connects us to our inner wisdom and intuition. Our ancient ancestors needed all their senses (sight, hearing, touch, taste and smell) plus their sixth sense (intuition) simply to survive. Animals still use this extra sense but most of us have forgotten how to. Your third eye chakra can help you to fine tune your sixth sense in the modern world. It can warn you of danger, save a lot of time (a flash of insight produces far quicker results than wading through a pile of data) and bring a beautiful spiritual awareness into your life.

- Meditate with your eyes closed. Focus on the middle of your forehead – if images come up, notice them and let them go. If they are important you will remember them afterward anyway, so don't worry about them.

- Ask a question, and then do something else – go for a walk, have a bath, chop the vegetables for supper... See if the answer, or a pattern, comes up spontaneously from your intuition.

- Keep a dream diary. Write down what you saw in your dreams, and look it up in a dream dictionary. There may be several different interpretations – many of them wild and wacky – but you will know when something makes sense to you.

- Be aware of coincidences, or of words or images that keep coming up. If songs keep running around your head, notice what the words are saying.

- Buy some oracle cards or consult the I Ching, the ancient Chinese manual of divination. The beauty of this method is that the images and words can be interpreted in different ways. None of them are right in an absolute sense, but they can stimulate your intuition and give you a message that is correct for you at the time (horoscopes can work the same way).

- Learn to see auras. Ask a friend to sit in front of a greyish wall, then dim the lighting (or use candles). If you unfocus your eyes, you might see an outline of white or bluish energy around them, which is a layer of their physical energy. With practice, you may be able to see other colours, too.

- Look out for spiritual signs. Concentrate on the good ones that make you feel happy. When I was first told I was going to be a healer, over the next week I saw signs connected to angels almost everywhere. I felt strongly drawn into a tacky gift shop and couldn't work out what I was doing there, until I looked up and saw magnificent angel wrapping paper all over the wall behind the till. Two people gave me little angels as presents. A child gave me a feather. I found another fluffy feather (for the first and only time) in my cup of tea. None of these signs meant much on their own, but I couldn't ignore how many of them there were, or how uplifted they made me feel.

- If you have a hunch that you've got a problem – a ghost in the house, or a health issue – check it out with your logical brain and see if you can solve it. If that niggling feeling won't go away, ask for help from a professional. So many of my healing clients start their session with "I know this sounds silly, but..."

REALLY, TRULY LOOK

As you work your way through the chakras, you've probably been using your eyes a lot, to spot the different rainbow colours. With this chakra, make an extra effort to notice what else you can see.

o Visit art galleries and look at paintings, both from a distance and close up.

o Go to an art shop, and admire the beautiful range of colours in a box of pencils or watercolour pastels.

o Go out into nature and look – really look – at leaves, flowers or the patterns on bark.

o Notice light: how it changes through the day and ripples through water.

o Get hold of a book of optical illusions.

o Look at mandalas – circular figures representing the universe. I particularly like Kathy Klein's modern mandalas made out of flowers on her Danmala website.

o Be grateful for all the beautiful things you see.

SEE BEAUTY EVERYWHERE

Even if you are stuck in heavy traffic, in an ugly part of town, you can still find beauty if you look for it. My friend, the journalist Lesley Garner, has a brilliant tip called "The Navajo Beauty Way" in her book *Everything I've Ever Done That Worked*. Here is a small taste of it, but do read the full version if you can:

Next time you find yourself bored and uncomfortable in solid traffic, try looking in each direction in turn and saying to yourself:

o "There is beauty ABOVE me". Look up, and you might notice the high white clouds racing across the sky.

o "There is beauty BEFORE me". You might notice the rich, fiery red of the tail lights on the van in front of you, or the sun reflected in the windows of a building.

o "There is beauty to the LEFT of me". For the first time see that the car in the next lane is a shimmering abstract of reflections, a dark gleam of high-gloss paintwork, a slick of mirror and chrome.

- "There is beauty to the RIGHT of me". Notice a play of light and colours on reflective surfaces as the traffic streams past.

- "There is beauty BELOW me". Look down at the folded fabric of clothes on your lap, the subtle textures, the little canyons of light and shade that form in the pleats and creases.

- "There is beauty BEHIND me". You might notice a curving chain of lights in your rear-view mirror... abstraction of lights and tones, geometric shapes and subtle curves.

- "There is beauty INSIDE me. My anger and frustration have been transformed by the exercise of looking."

- "There is beauty all AROUND me. Yes there is. Thank you."

REMOVE VISUAL CLUTTER

Set the intention that you want to have clear vision, by cleaning your windows and mirrors and giving your reading glasses a good polish.

Is there any distracting visual clutter that you don't like to see, such as piles of old jars and packets in your kitchen? Put it away, and keep the few items that you love or need in plain sight.

Are there any objects in your house that you have forgotten to look at for a while? When was the last time you really appreciated that picture on your wall or the postcard on your desk?

PLAN AHEAD, GET PERSPECTIVE

When your third eye is working well, you know where you
are going in life and what you want to achieve. But if your
long-term plans are a bit hazy, try making a vision board.
Find a stack of old magazines and cut out pictures and
phrases that inspire you. Put the board up on the wall,
and use it to focus your intention. According to books like
The Secret by Rhonda Byrne, when you make your goals
visible, all sorts of opportunities and helpful people will
suddenly become visible, too.

You could also do a little visualization. Imagine yourself at
your own funeral, and see your friends and family giving
eulogies about you. What do they say? What else would
you like them to say? If the answers touch or inspire you,
it's probably your soul showing you where it wants you to
go next.

Third Eye Chakra Meditation

HOW TO MEET YOUR GUIDE

We have a team of guides, angels and ancestors looking after us. It must be a frustrating job, because on the whole we don't listen to them. Often they have to resort to showing us information in our dreams, or subtly drawing our attention to coincidences. If we make the effort to connect with them, through our third eye, then communication with them can become easier.

o Lie down comfortably. Breathe IN to your lower stomach, and each time you breathe OUT, relax a part of your body, from your feet to your head. Ask your protective guides and guardians to move in closely around you while you go on a visual journey.

o Take your mind's eye to a long, empty beach. You are standing at one end and can see the curve of the shore, with the sea on one side coming into the land. You are setting this up so that the beach is very peaceful and safe. You can hear the sound of the waves and feel the crunch of the sand under your feet as you walk.

o At the other end of the beach you can see a distant figure. They are walking toward you. You feel a sense of recognition, familiarity and anticipation. As they come closer, the light is shining behind them, so that you can see the outline and the light all around them, but not yet their face.

o Look down – perhaps you can see their feet. What kind of shoes are they wearing? Bring your gaze up. What kind of clothes are they wearing? What colour, what texture? As your gaze reaches their face, it may still be blurred, but the blur is clearing and you can make out some features. The figure gently holds out their hand to you, and you feel the beautiful energy around it.

o Just above the beach is a bench, looking over the sea. You walk over together and sit down on it. The figure has something for you in their hands. It is a gift, and you may need to unwrap it. You can put it in your pocket or wrap it around you. The guide may have some words for you. Lean a little closer. Can you hear them? Or do you get a sense of what they mean.

o You feel the loving energy emanating from this guide as you say goodbye. You know you will be able to call on this figure, and meet them again, when you need them.

o As you say goodbye, the guide walks back along the beach and you turn back the way you came; your body feels heavy and you begin to have a sense that you are passing back through the mists, back into your own room, back into your own body.

o Wiggle your fingers and toes, and stretch out. When you are ready, open your eyes and write down anything that you would like to remember.

Crown
Chakra

Ancient Sanskrit name	Sahasrara (meaning: thousand-petalled)
Commonly known as	Crown chakra, violet-white chakra
Number	Seven, the seventh and highest of the main chakras
Location	Top of the head – a single chakra, pointing upward
Associations	Connection to the divine, and to the divinity within you
Related organs	Top of the brain, pituitary gland
Sense	Awareness
Element	Cosmic energy
Age	43–49 and 92–98
When in balance	Spirituality; a feeling of connection, but also of benign detachment; sense of euphoria, wonder, calm, spaciousness and light; life has meaning
When weak or damaged	Feeling of being cut off from spirituality or hostile to it; sensation of meaninglessness; loneliness and depression
When over-developed	Disconnection from reality; delusion or religious fanaticism
Symbol/yantra	A thousand-petalled lotus; the number of petals can also represent infinity
Phrases	I am divine, I am connected, I know
Crystals	Try clear crystal quartz or amethyst, to clear your mind and enhance feelings of spirituality

I trust that
the universe is
supporting me

I am
interested
in spiritual
subjects

I believe in a
higher power
(though I don't
necessarily
call it God)

I definitely
believe in
good energy

Prayer or
meditation is an
important part
of my life

I am more
interested in ideas
than in practical
matters

Sometimes
it's hard being
a spirit in a
human body

I've had
glimpses of
a deeper
reality

Music, art
or beauty
can help me
soar upward

I love inspiring
quotes, books
and people

I believe that
everything in
the universe
is connected

I believe
in life
after death

I am
evolving

Cleaning my
energy and
purifying my
soul are very
important to me

Sometimes
I'm a bit
spacey and
ungrounded

I am Connected

In the journey up through the chakras, the crown chakra is like the top of a mountain, where the air is incredibly pure and clear. This chakra points upward from the top of the head and has the finest and lightest vibration of all seven chakras. If it had a note, it might sound like the clear chime of a tuning fork or a silver bell.

I love putting my hand above someone's head and tuning into their crown chakra. When it is working well, it feels LUMINOUS AND ETHEREAL, which makes me feel UPLIFTED AND INSPIRED. Saints and mystics are often painted with a corona or halo of light, but the rest of us have one, too.

The crown chakra has two important jobs. The first is to CONNECT us with the sacred energy above. Depending on your belief system, you may call this God, a higher power or the highest point of light. The second is to connect us to the divinity within ourselves and make us aware of our eternal, spiritual aspect, which you might call your SOUL, SPIRIT OR HIGHER SELF.

According to spiritual teachers, when the crown chakra connects us to both these aspects of divinity, something amazing can happen. It can be the portal to a HIGHER STATE OF CONSCIOUSNESS, where we realize that we are connected to absolutely everything in the cosmos. They say that enlightenment occurs when a wave realizes it is part of the ocean, and that there are no boundaries between it and all the other water molecules in the sea. They say that separation is just an illusion, and that when you achieve connection you can experience BLISS.

In this state you know that your soul is PURE LIGHT. You can connect with infinite wisdom across past, present and future. Time doesn't really exist. Distance is immaterial. Everything is part of the great whole.

If you are very SPIRITUAL, you may already have a sense of what this means. But most of us only start to get glimpses of enlightenment as our soul unfolds over a lifetime.

Working up through the chakras can accelerate the process. A flourishing, fully evolved crown chakra is connected to all the chakras, but particularly to the base...the more deeply rooted we are, the higher we can soar.

In this journey upward, we are now on the top floor of the lighthouse, and as we bring everything together from all our chakras, the colours merge in a beautiful beam of pure white light.

When the
Crown Chakra is Balanced

When the crown chakra is spinning well, the world can seem a GLORIOUS, HARMONIOUS place. When spiritual energy is flowing in and out of this chakra, you might regularly feel WONDER AND AWE, have a sense of your higher purpose on earth or find MEANING in almost everything you do.

You might feel a DEEP SENSE OF TRUST that a higher power is looking after you, in the same way that you trust the sun will rise every morning or there is always blue sky if you go high enough beyond the clouds.

You might often feel a sense of UNCONDITIONAL LOVE AND COMPASSION. Though you will recognize this feeling from the heart chakra, in the crown chakra it has moved up a notch. It is more detached, but more universal – a feeling of compassion for everyone and everything.

When your crown chakra is healthy, you know there are many, many different paths to TRUE CONNECTION and compassion, and you respect them all.

Recognizing when the
Crown
Chakra is Weak or Damaged

When nothing much is flowing through this chakra, you can feel disconnected from your spirituality. If NOTHING INSPIRES YOU particularly, life can feel flat, grey and meaningless. You may never get the sense of being lifted up, or of going beyond ordinary existence into something bigger. If you feel DISCONNECTED FROM EVERYTHING – including yourself – you can become LONELY and DEPRESSED.

But this isn't always the case. If your lower chakras are highly developed, you might be working hard, earning money, eating large meals, getting drunk, having sex, pursuing fame, buying stuff or whatever else fills up your time, without a clue that you are missing out on anything. You might do very well materially, because you aren't bothered by moral scruples and DON'T GET DISTRACTED BY SOUL-SEARCHING. Because you can't experience spiritual connection yourself, you might think spiritual people are odd or deluded, and congratulate yourself for living in the real world. However, you might have a STRONG FEAR OF DEATH and secretly envy their certainty.

Why would a crown chakra be weak? It may be a simple question of physiology. MRI scans show that atheists and believers have slightly different brain structures. Upbringing can have a lot to do with it, too; you may never have been given the opportunity to explore spiritual topics, or were laughed at for bringing them up. If you were made to attend boring religious services as a child, or were badly treated by people who claimed to have religious authority over you, this can make you HOSTILE TO THE IDEA OF GOD.

In some people, the crown chakra isn't damaged; it just hasn't had the chance to unfold yet. These people have many other responsibilities, such as building a career or taking care of their children. When they are older and have more time for themselves, these people may spontaneously begin to feel a sense of the connection.

Recognizing when the
Crown
Chakra is Over-developed

When there is too much energy flowing in and out of your crown chakra, you might FIND ORDINARY LIFE VERY DIFFICULT. With your head in the clouds, you might be full of high ideals and complicated philosophy, but they aren't much use if you can hardly boil an egg.

You may be baffled by popular culture, but still soak up anxieties from the collective unconscious. These can swirl around in the atmosphere as thought forms. When there is, say, a major election, or terror attack, my clients carry far more energy than usual around their heads: they pick up on things that everyone is worrying about.

If your third eye chakra is also wide open, you might be DELUGED BY PSYCHIC EXPERIENCES. With your head full of visions, you might feel disconnected from reality or mentally unbalanced. Being devoutly religious can be beautiful and nourishing, but not if you neglect to take care of yourself or cut yourself off from the world.

What causes the crown chakra to open too wide? You can become UNBALANCED if you spend too much time thinking and not taking care of your physical body. If you are easily hurt, or have suffered trauma, it might feel safer to DISSOCIATE FROM YOUR BODY and stay up in your head. Fantasy may feel better than reality and more trustworthy than human emotions.

Mind-altering drugs can also blow your crown chakra wide open. They are definitely not a safe fast track to true enlightenment. Instead, it is better to strengthen and stabilize all your chakras, until eventually the thousand-petalled lotus on the top of your head blooms in its own good time.

WHAT HAPPENS TO OVERALL FLOW IF THE CROWN CHAKRA ISN'T BALANCED?

If this chakra is underpowered, then inspiring schemes won't be flowing down into your lower chakras. If your lower chakras are working well, you will get stuff done, but it will be pretty mundane and basic, because the divine spark will be missing.

If the crown chakra is overpowered, so that you are top-heavy, you might find it very hard to start anything or keep it going, let alone complete it. Great ideas to change the world might be running around your head for years, but unless you can inspire someone else to take them on, they might never happen.

Case Study

WHEN THE CROWN CHAKRA OPENS TOO QUICKLY

Jess was backpacking around South America on her gap year before university with two friends, and as they were open-minded and spiritually curious, they decided to go to an ayahuasca ceremony in Colombia.

"We were staying in a hostel and there were leaflets lying around, and some other backpackers said it was an interesting experience.

They said ayahuasca wasn't addictive, that people had been using it for thousands of years and that the Colombians called it a "teacher drug", because it gave you such beautiful visions. We loved the idea of seeing some psychedelic stuff and coming home wiser. It would be an experience.

"Unfortunately, I don't think we found a proper shaman. I drank a cup of really nasty liquid and then I was very sick. I did see quite a lot, but it was horrible – like a nightmare. I felt out of control. At one point I was waving my arms around and scratching my own face.

"Maybe I was lucky; I heard stories afterward of girls being raped in that kind of situation. I don't want to repeat anything like that again. I still feel a bit shaky when I think about it. I blame myself for going into something like that so blindly.

"At uni, I went to some yoga classes and joined a meditation group. And I am interested in going on a retreat one day. Maybe something opened up – who knows? But I want to tread slowly."

How to Heal the
Crown Chakra

As always, the suggestions on the following pages are meant to inspire. So connect with the ones that are right for you now.

Because the crown chakra has such a high vibration, most of these suggestions are energetic rather than practical, and their focus is on opening up or balancing this chakra.

If your crown chakra needs calming down instead, go back to the base chakra chapter starting on page 26 (and possibly some of the other chapters), then come back to the crown chakra exercises later.

Focus on
VIOLET-WHITE

Pale violet has the highest vibration of the seven colours of the rainbow. But the crown chakra can also be associated with pure white, which has all the chakra rainbow colours within it. To remind you of the crown chakra, look out mainly for things that are white; and if you see a flash of pale violet as well, that is a bonus. Because crown chakra energy has such a high, fine vibration, you could also look out for crystalline structures and for light itself.

Try wearing white clothes over all your chakras, such as a white shirt during the day or white pyjamas at night. If you want to focus only on the crown chakra, maybe you could find a white or violet-coloured cap or something to wear in your hair (double points for their location). Notice how much white there is around you: white paintwork, fluffy clouds, your bathtub, white plates, the plain paper of the pages in a book. You might see pale violet at dawn and sunset, and lots of different flowers in both of these colours.

You could make a little altar, or post pictures of white or violet items (or even of angels) on social media.

Feed your
Crown Chakra

Keep eating purple food (*see* page 138) or switch to delicious, healthy white food, which can be full of nutrients such as anthoxanthin, allicin and quercetin.

Try vegetables such as cauliflower, cabbage, fennel, mushrooms, white truffles, garlic, shallots, the white parts of leeks, parsnips, white asparagus, white beans, chickpeas, beansprouts and tofu.

Lots of fruit and vegetables are white on the inside, such as apples, pears, lychees, custard apples, dragon fruit, guavas, yams, Jerusalem artichokes and white nectarines and peaches, Others can be both white and purple, including onions, mottled aubergines, purple cabbage and turnips.

Eat grains and nuts: rice, white corn (including popcorn and polenta), oats (including porridge), wheat (including bread and pasta), tapioca, white quinoa, coconut, macadamia, cashew, Brazil and pine nuts.

Also dairy foods: milk, yogurt, kefir, cream, white butter, white cheese such as feta; and nondairy foods, such as coconut yogurt and cashew cheese.

Remind yourself to focus on the crown chakra when eating airy food – such as a mousse or meringue – or anything sweet: ambrosia, nectar and manna all have sacred associations and are meant to be sweet.

You could also try focusing on the crown chakra by fasting occasionally. If you are physically up to this, fasting can be good for your body and can give you a feeling of lightness and clarity.

Heal your
Physical Body

Look out for any activities that focus attention on the top of your head.

GET A HEAD START

The simplest way to connect with your body through the top of your head is by brushing or washing your hair.

You could also try an Indian head massage or, better still, a craniosacral treatment, which works on the energy around your head and down your spine.

TAKE IT OUTSIDE

Whenever you can, try to exercise outdoors. While you are there, bring your attention to the top of your head. Be aware of sunshine or rain reaching this part of your body first. If it's cloudy, remember that there is blue sky up there somewhere, and imagine reaching up from the top of your head to find it.

For balance, it is important to incorporate some grounding exercises, too; perhaps the easiest one is to think about the soles of your feet touching the ground as you walk or move around.

COSMIC CONNECTION BREATHING

The atoms in our body are incredibly old; they connect us back into time. The hydrogen atoms that we breathe in were formed 13 billion years ago during the Big Bang. They have travelled through space to get here, and on this earth they have been part of rocks, water and air. They also connect us with other people. Scientists have calculated that every time we breathe in, we are almost certainly breathing in one or two molecules that were breathed out by Julius Caesar, Shakespeare or any other historical figure you care to mention. This meditation focuses on those connections.

1 As you breathe IN think –
   "I am breathing in connection".

2 As you breathe OUT think –
   "I am breathing out connection".

3 As you breathe IN think –
   "I am breathing in the universe".

4 As you breathe OUT think –
   "I am breathing out the universe".

Tune into your
Crown Chakra

The crown chakra is associated with the element of cosmic energy. This section is about deepening your spiritual connection.

Humans have been struggling for thousands of years to express what it means to experience a divine connection. Here are four different methods that you can use to try to gain a sense of it...

1. BOOST YOUR SPIRITUAL CONNECTION

Here are some words that make me feel uplifted:

- The divine, the source, the highest point of light, heaven, celestial, elysian, heavenly, angelic; light, luminescence, radiance, clear, crystalline, pellucid, translucent; peace, calm, love, gratitude, inspiration, joy, wonder, euphoria, rapture, ecstasy, bliss; spiritual journey, awakening, raised consciousness, high vibration, transcendence, enlightenment, nirvana; the soul, the spirit, blessings, Namaste.

Do any of these words work for you? If you find pictures are more potent, what kind of images inspire you and give you a sense of transcendence and connection?

2. EXPERIENCE SPIRITUALITY

Here are some ways we may encourage our crown chakra to bloom and open up to spiritual experience:

- Religious practice: Many religions have worked out how to stimulate the senses using prayer and ritual. Visit a Gothic cathedral that draws your eyes upward toward God; a Hindu temple full of incense and icons; a Buddhist stupa with bells and chanting or a Native American drumming circle under the stars.

- Tapping into other vibrations: When you meditate with other people, you can get into a meditative state more quickly. You can also tap into spiritual vibrations by visiting places where other people have been inspired for centuries, such as the pilgrim path to Santiago de Compostela in northern Spain.

- Art and music: You can connect with spirituality though art in all its forms – listening to music, going to galleries or reading poetry (particularly by mystics such as Rumi). Just be aware that this can be strong stuff: Stendhal syndrome, or Florence syndrome, is a recognized medical condition – symptoms of which include a rapid heartbeat, dizziness, fainting and even hallucinations – that can occur when people are exposed to too much great or spiritual art.

- Nature: Climb a mountain or hill so that you can see for miles. Try staring up at a sky full of stars; a dawn sunrise; shafts of light coming through clouds; or the Northern or Southern Lights. Flowers and trees can be inspiring, too. As the English poet Elizabeth Barrett Browning put it, "Earth's crammed with heaven, and every common bush afire with God."

3. CONNECT WITH YOURSELF (AND IT CAN BE HARD)

o   Ground, centre and be present: You can open up your crown chakra by being fully aware and present in everything you do. It doesn't matter if you aren't a yoga teacher or a mystic. If you are, say, a gardener, computer programmer or painter and you can notice what you are doing, see beauty and a deeper reality, then you are on a spiritual path.

o   Be brave: The Swiss psychoanalyst Carl Jung said there is no coming to consciousness without pain. People will do anything, no matter how absurd, to avoid facing their own soul. "One does not become enlightened by imagining figures of light, but by making the darkness conscious."

o   See higher purpose, and lessons in every situation: Life lessons are there to teach you, until you are no longer triggered. As Buddha said, "Every experience, no matter how bad it seems, holds within it a blessing of some kind. The goal is to find it."

o   Be quiet: Work hard at committing yourself to periods of doing absolutely nothing (even for five minutes, or once a year on holiday).

o   Reiki attunement: If you have ever received some Reiki healing, you will know what a celestial experience it can be. Reiki healing comes from a very high, divine place. You can get attuned to this frequency yourself (rather like tuning a radio) by going on a Reiki course.

4. MASTER MEDITATION

If you've been dodging the meditations in this book, then I sympathize, because I used to dodge around meditation, too. Whenever I tried it, I didn't get anywhere near the peaceful state of mind everyone talked about. I just assumed that meditation wasn't for me.

My "Aha" moment was reading *Eat, Pray, Love* by the American author Elizabeth Gilbert, and particularly her vivid description of trying to meditate in an Indian ashram. It was reassuring to know how incredibly hard it was for her to wrestle with her monkey mind, and inspiring to read about how she got there in the end.

Meditation (or mindfulness, which basically means focusing on one thing at a time) is extremely good for the crown chakra. If you are lucky you can connect spiritually, whether you are riding a bicycle, playing with your children or commuting to work on the train. If you can already feel it, that is great – carry on. For the rest of us, the mind is usually too noisy to feel spiritual. That monkey brain is whooping and swinging about all over the place, full of anxiety, questions, reminders of things we ought to be doing in the future, and random memories and rehashes of the past.

Meditation is a tool to quieten this monkey, by focusing on one thing at a time. As we breathe or walk (or whatever), we get the chance to step back and realize that our thoughts aren't us, and that we have a choice not to be overwhelmed by them. Detachment simply means having the ability to access this quiet spot, where we can observe our thoughts from a distance and let them go. Eventually it gets easier and easier. And this is where the magic happens: when we become detached, it's so quiet and calm that we have a good chance of becoming aware of our divine connection.

Meditation isn't the only way to open your crown chakra, but it's definitely worth trying. The good news is that there are many different kinds of meditation. Counting your breaths, saying a mantra, walking, gazing at a candle, dancing (think of the whirling dervishes), concentrating on your yoga practice – anything, really, where you only think of one thing at a time. The meditation on page 167 is particularly focused on the crown chakra.

Crown Chakra Meditation

CONNECTING WITH THE LIGHT

I often encourage clients to do this visualization for themselves during a healing session. It is very nourishing and uplifting. Even people who have never done this kind of work, and aren't confident about their abilities, usually have super-sparkly crown chakras at the end of it. The energy above their head feels expansive and much brighter. The more often I have felt this kind of energetic shift with my hands, the more convinced I become that energy really can flow where thought goes.

o Sit or lie comfortably. Take some slow, deep breaths and use your OUT breath to relax each part of your body in turn, starting with your feet.

o Bring your attention up to the crown of your head, and set the intention to connect with the highest point of light (God, the divine, the angelic realm or whatever you want to call it). Ask for a big beam of pure white light to come down onto your crown chakra. It is already pure, but as it touches your crown it becomes even purer – exactly the vibration and energy your body needs.

o As you breathe IN, imagine this light coming inside your head, filling it up. Then flowing down into your neck and shoulders and into your arms and hands.

o Come back to your crown chakra, and notice that the light is still flowing, as much as you need. Breathe it down into your chest and lungs, and around your heart. Breathe it down into your stomach and onward. You can trust that this light knows where to go, though all the twists of your digestive organs, nourishing and healing them.

o Come back to your crown chakra – the beautiful light is still flowing. Bring it all the way down the back of your spine, through each vertebra, and down into your hipbones, pelvis and legs. You are filling up with light: you are glowing.

o If there is anything that the light needs to dissolve, it can carry this away through your feet and down into the earth. But most of the light stays in your body to nourish you and make you shine. See, or feel, what this is like.

o Now gently come back to the top of your head, and ask the light beam to withdraw gently, back up to where it came from. Thank it as it goes.

o When you are ready, wriggle your fingers and toes and open your eyes.

(To balance, you could also do the Root Meditation. *See* page 44.)

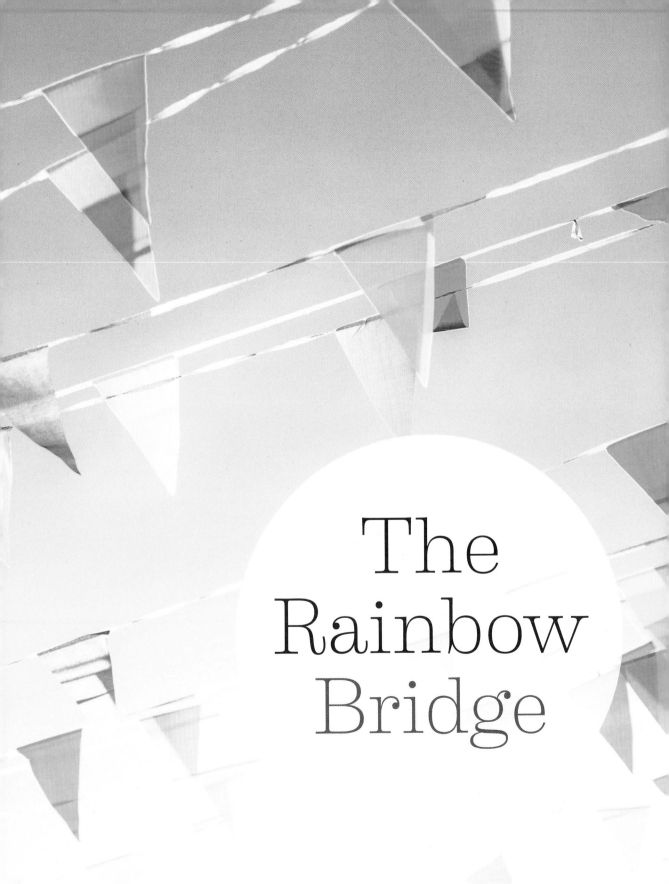

The
Rainbow
Bridge

Harmonizing the seven
Chakras

When each one of the chakras is balanced and working together, it's like a full orchestra in harmony: the sound is rich, and none of the instruments dominates. Here are three techniques to work all the chakras together. When they are harmonized it is like making a beautiful rainbow bridge within your body, connecting matter and spirit, earth and sky.

TECHNIQUE 1

Chakras feel much happier when the energy flows properly between them. They can support and strengthen each other, which makes life feel much easier. Think of a wind instrument – perhaps a child's recorder or a smooth jazz saxophone. The air flows in through the top and down through the instrument to make a sound. You can play a tune by opening or closing different air holes with your fingers. Our energy field does something similar: energy flows up and down through our body, and in and out through our chakras. When all our chakras are working, we feel fully alive. If any of our chakras are blocked, then our expression – the range of tunes we can play – is limited. So just as musicians clean and adjust their instruments to keep them in tune, we need to clean up our energy field and our chakras. Here is a quick, simple way to connect and balance them.

Connecting your chakras

○ Start at the base. Put one hand over your base chakra, and the other hand over your sacral chakra. Set the intention to connect them together, with your hands as jump-leads. You may or may not be able to feel anything, but stay in this position for about a minute.

○ Then work your way up, gently connecting each chakra to the one above it (the sacral to the solar plexus, the solar plexus to the heart, and so on), until you reach your third eye and crown chakras.

○ Finish by connecting the crown and base chakras.

TECHNIQUE 2

Chakras can suck in all sorts of energy. From other people's sadness to the general draining blah that you can pick up on a busy shopping street or on the train. If you feel tired and grouchy at the end of the day, cleaning up all your chakras can make you feel better immediately. This process is very simple.

Cleansing your chakras

o Step into the shower.

o As the water touches your skin and washes you physically, imagine that a beam of light is also pouring down to wash your entire auric field and all of your chakras, washing you energetically (or simply ask it to do so).

o As you clean away old, stale energy in this way, it can feel like taking a heavy load off your back. You may find that you have more energy and can deal with any problems with a clearer head and a lighter touch.

TECHNIQUE 3

Spotting chakra colours is a very good way to remind you of particular chakras (I hope that you have enjoyed all those rainbow-coloured vegetables as much as I do). Colour breathing takes this one step farther, by bringing all those beautiful rainbow shades into your body, one after another, to nourish all your chakras from the inside.

Colour breathing

o Lie comfortably on your back. As you breathe IN, imagine that you can breathe in through the whole of the front of your body, as though you are drawing oxygen in through the pores of your skin.

o Now imagine that you are connecting with a gentle, beautiful, glowing red energy – the essence of red, the highest point of red light. Visualize this soft red light flowing gently into the front of your body with each IN breath, moving like vapour into every cell. Allow it to warm and heal your body, then ask the colour to flow into your groin, just above your base chakra, and to concentrate itself as a lovely ball of soft red light.

o Repeat with orange energy, bringing it into every part of your body in the same way, and then concentrating itself into your sacral area. Then do the same for all the other colours: yellow (solar plexus), green (heart), blue (throat), purple (third eye) and finishing with violet-white in your crown.

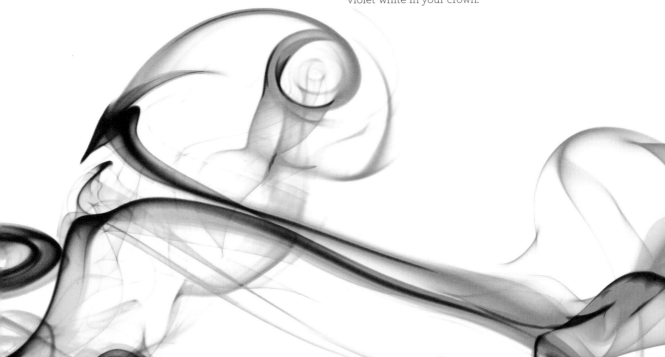

Working with
Crystals

Chakras vibrate, and so do crystals. Good crystals can amplify chakra energy work and strengthen their energy.

CHOOSING YOUR CRYSTALS

There are so many different recommendations for chakra crystals that it can become confusing. My advice is not to rely on descriptions, and not to order online. Instead, go to a crystal shop and try out some crystals for yourself, by physically picking them up. You will get a sense that some crystals feel wrong in your hands, while others feel good and will work well with you.

At the beginning, keep it simple, by sticking to the corresponding chakra colours. With experience you might wish to swap them around and try other crystals.

A shortlist to start you off:

o **Base chakra** – red jasper.

o **Sacral chakra** – orange carnelian.

o **Solar plexus chakra** – yellow citrine.

o **Heart chakra** – green aventurine or rose-pink quartz.

o **Throat chakra** – sky-blue angelite.

o **Third eye chakra** – purple amethyst.

o **Crown chakra** – clear quartz.

In addition you could try:

o Clear quartz – choose an extra one which can work with all the chakras and enhance other stones.

o Black tourmaline – which is good for grounding.

CARING FOR YOUR CRYSTALS

Crystals are like pets: they need looking after. If you are kind to them, they will work harder for you. They can also absorb vibrations from working with the chakras, so clean them regularly by washing them in water or burying them in earth; and recharge them by leaving them in sunlight or moonlight for a while.

USING YOUR CRYSTALS

If you are working on one particular chakra, hold the relevant crystal in your hands. Tune in, by focusing on the colour and how it makes you feel, then place it over the chakra in question. Set your intention for the crystal: do you want it to open up that chakra, calm it down or balance it?

For a full chakra crystal healing, lie down and place each of the crystals on the appropriate chakras on your body. Place the black tourmaline at your feet, for extra grounding. Connect with the crystal energy for 10–30 minutes, then remove the crystals in the same order.

During the day, you can tuck crystals into your pocket (or down your bra, if you wear one). They don't need to be right over the appropriate chakra. Don't wear them for too long, though, particularly at first, because crystal energy can be strong.

Working with
Essential Oils

Essential oils can also work very powerfully with your chakras. Below is a shortlist of suggestions, based on the colours and attributes of different oils. However, your sense of smell is very personal and will be linked to your unique memories, so do follow your own nose.

CHOOSING ESSENTIAL OILS

o **Base chakra** – calming rose (think of red roses) or a woody oil such as sandalwood, for grounding.

o **Sacral chakra** – neroli (the scent of orange-bearing trees) or ylang-ylang, both of which are very light and sensuous.

o **Solar plexus chakra** – stimulating lemon or soothing chamomile (for their colour), or vetiver to reduce anxiety.

o **Heart chakra** – rose (think of pink roses), helichrysum for a broken heart or palo santo to reconnect with stuck emotions.

o **Throat chakra** – ethereal blue lotus (for its colour) or eucalyptus to open up your throat.

o **Third eye chakra** – lavender (for its colour) or bay laurel to open up your sixth sense.

o **Crown chakra** – uplifting jasmine (white flowers) or frankincense, which is seen as a holy oil and can be good for meditation.

If you prefer, you could choose just one oil that you like and use it for all the chakras. Rose and lavender are particularly useful; they are known as adaptogenic oils, as they can work in many different ways.

USING ESSENTIAL OILS

Unless you know what you are doing, always dilute essential oils before you use them, with water or a neutral carrier oil such as jojoba. Breathe in the scent before you apply it, and really focus on cleaning, opening up or balancing whichever chakras you are healing.

You could put a few drops into a spray bottle of water (the type used for ironing or to mist plants) or into the bath, for a nice long chakra soak. My favourite method is an electric aromatherapy diffuser, which sends out puffs of scented water vapour – it's a nice light way to bring the energy of the oils into your aura (and it makes the room smell good, too).

If you want to apply an essential oil directly onto a chakra, add a few drops of it to a neutral carrier oil. Breathe in the scent, set your intention, then rub a little of the diluted oil directly onto the chakra in question – not forgetting the back of your body, if you can reach it. But don't put essential oil on your base chakra, as this is a super-sensitive area. Rub the oil into your feet or onto your lower back instead.

If you are working on all the chakras and you don't mind splashing out on seven different oils, you can apply them in a slow and mindful ritual, one for each chakra. Gently breathe in the scent before you apply it, and be sure to concentrate your attention on each chakra in turn.

Yoga for
Chakras

Yoga has been linked to the chakras for thousands of years. It can strengthen your body, soothe your emotions, calm down your brain and connect you to your spirituality.

WHICH POSES TO CHOOSE?

There are so many different yoga poses, and so many different suggestions about which pose works for which chakra, that I'm going to keep it very simple. Rather than make a list of perfect postures for every chakra, my advice is to find a general yoga class that suits you. Then watch out for these four chakra clues:

Movement

When you flex, stretch or strengthen a particular part of the body, you will also be working on the chakra in that area (for example, hip stretches can open up and balance your sacral chakra).

Touch

If you touch a particular chakra, you can stimulate it (for instance, you might feel a little buzz around your crown chakra after doing a headstand).

Attention

If you focus your awareness on a particular chakra, you will be bringing energy to it (for example, in the Cobra pose you might first notice the physical sensation in your lower back, but you can also bring attention to your throat and heart chakras as you stretch the front of your body).

Ground and uplift

Notice which parts of your body are in contact with the floor and which are stretching upward, to remind yourself that chakras are like stepping stones between earth and heaven (for example, in the Warrior pose, notice how your feet ground you and your arms are reaching skyward).

Simple yoga stretches to do at home

You can balance all of your chakras using the simple yoga stretches that are described on the following pages.

Gently try at least one exercise from each of the following four categories, so that your chakra energy flows beautifully in all directions:

1   Up and down

2   Forward and backward

3   Side-to-side

4   The Big Shake

The sequence could take you less than ten minutes and set you up for a very good day. Repeat each movement several times.

1 Up and down

These exercises increase the flow of energy between your chakras and connect them to each other.

Drawing a circle

This is a very simple way to bring awareness to all seven chakras.

o   Stand with your feet hip-width apart.

o   Breathe IN and lift your arms out to the sides. Keep moving them upward until your hands touch high above your head and you have made a wide circle.

o   Breathe OUT and lower your arms to the sides. Keep moving them downward until your hands touch in front of your body and you have made a wide circle.

o   Repeat.

When you get used to making the circles, focus on the energy running up and down between your chakras, as you move your arms.

Earth and heaven

This pose connects you to the ground and sky.

o   As you breathe IN – stand up tall and stretch your arms up to the sky.

o   As you breathe OUT – bend your knees into a squat and touch the floor.

o   Repeat.

When you get used to the movement of this pose, bring your awareness to the flow of energy up and down between your chakras.

2 Forward and backward

These poses increase the flow of energy in and out of each individual chakra.

The cat / Cow pose

This flexes your spine and brings awareness into the front and back of each chakra.

- Start on your hands and knees, with your back flat like a tabletop.

- As you breathe OUT, tuck your head and tailbone in, so that your back is arched upward like an angry cat and the middle of your back is closer to the ceiling.

- As you breathe IN, pull your head and tailbone up, so that the middle of your back is arched downward and the front of your tummy is closer to the floor.

- Repeat.

Standing spinal stretch

This is like the Cat pose, except that you are standing up and using your arms as well.

- As you breathe IN, look up and stick your tailbone out so that your back is arched. Stretch your open arms out sideways. This is a beautiful, generous pose to open the front of your chakras.

- As you breathe OUT, look down and tuck in your bottom, so that your back is rounded. Bring your arms around you to hug your body. This is a comforting pose to open out the back of your chakras.

- Repeat.

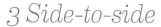

3 Side-to-side

Spiralling your spine from side to side is very beneficial for all your chakras. This movement can encourage your energy to flow between them and can also release blockages in individual chakras.

Sideways twist

This is a beautiful stretch and is much simpler to do in real life than to describe in words.

- Lie on your back, with your arms out to the sides in a T-shape and your legs flat on the floor.

- Slide the sole of your right foot along the floor, until it is level with your left knee. (Your right leg will be a triangle, with the knee pointing upward.)

- Keep your arms and shoulders on the floor, and turn your head over to the right. At the same time bring your right knee over toward the floor on your left. Hold for a few breaths.

- Repeat on the other side.

Windmill arms

This involves a similar sideways twisting movement, but standing up.

- Start with your feet hip-width apart and your knees slightly bent. Turn your head and shoulders round to the right. Let your arms be relaxed, so that they can move, too.

- Repeat on the other side, by turning your head and shoulders to the left.

When you get a nice rhythm going, you will find that your arms swing out loosely and freely in each twist. As you turn, the heel of the back foot will probably come off the floor too, so that you can twist slightly further.

4 The Big Shake

This posture is incredibly useful, as it shakes up all the energy in your body and in your chakras. It can calm you down if you are feeling tense (zebras do a big body shake after they've escaped from a predator, which brings down their stress hormones). You can also use it to shake other people's energy out of your auric field, and to perk up your own energy if you are feeling sluggish.

Shake it off

o   Start by standing with your feet flat on the ground, knees slightly bent.

o   Bounce gently on the balls of your feet to send a vibration up through your body.

o   Then focus on your knees and hips and intensify the movement.

o   Shake your wrists, as though you are shaking water off your hands, and work up through your elbows and shoulders to intensify this movement, too.

o   Shake your head as well, so that your whole body is moving, from your feet to your crown.

How
Chakras
can Help
your Flow

I am fascinated by people who can get things done. Whether it is effortlessly pulling together a good meal, getting their own business off the ground or setting up a project that helps others. Particularly the people who don't fuss, don't get stressed and don't exhaust themselves. How do they turn their ideas into reality and keep new projects flowing, when it is so easy to become stuck and scared?

In energy terms, it's about having clean, healthy chakras. If any are blocked, ideas get stuck and it's like walking uphill through mud to achieve anything.

LOCATING THE PROBLEM

If you have a really great idea but can't seem to make it happen, or can't seem to make it joyful, look at your bodily symptoms. If the project gives you a headache, a sore throat, heart palpitations, butterflies in your stomach or digestive problems, you've probably found the answer. Clear the chakra in question and life should get easier.

Every chakra is important, which is a good reminder to those of us on a spiritual path. It's no good having beautiful idealistic dreams if your lower chakras are weak and you can't make your business work or feed your family.

The flow of energy between our chakras goes both up and down. Over the next few pages we will look at the importance of flow and how each of your chakras can affect your life choices, develop your ideas and make them happen.

Downward flow

If you want to turn a brilliant idea into a physical reality,
the energy flows DOWNWARD from the crown chakra.
Here's how it could go:

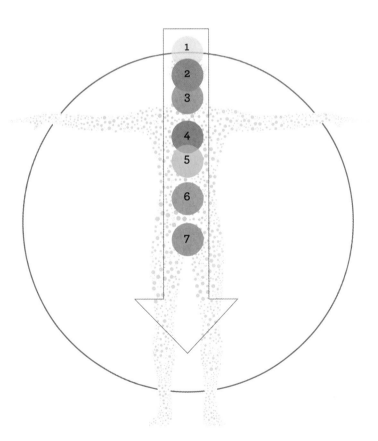

1 Crown Chakra
You feel inspired.

2 Third Eye Chakra
You get a glimpse of something, big
or small, that could work.

3 Throat Chakra
You start talking about it, to yourself
or others.

4 Heart Chakra
You begin to feel passionate about it.

5 Solar Plexus Chakra
You become determined to make
it happen.

6 Sacral Chakra
You incubate and germinate the project.

7 Base Chakra
You give birth to the idea, manifest it
and make it a reality.

Upward flow

If your physical reality is fine, but you trudge along
making money and never feel inspired or joyful, the flow
of chakra energy needs to go UPWARD from the base
chakra, to expand and lighten up. Here is how it might go:

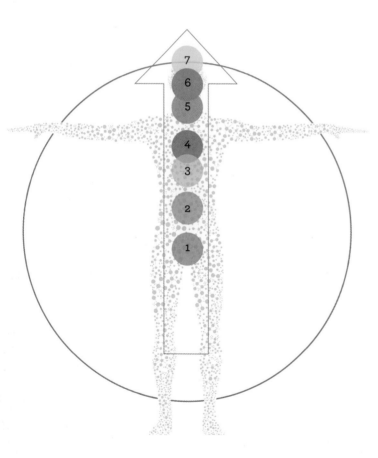

7 Crown Chakra
You begin to trust that there is a higher power
that will inspire you and show you the way forward.

6 Third Eye Chakra
You start to feel inspired, and you see far more
than you did before.

5 Throat Chakra
You start talking and, more importantly, you
start listening, and your ideas grow.

4 Heart Chakra
You get passionate about it; you may also start
connecting with other people.

3 Solar Plexus Chakra
You become more determined to reach for
a different kind of life.

2 Sacral Chakra
You start to feel that you would like to have more
pleasure and enjoy the fruits of your hard work.

1 Base Chakra
You begin to become aware that there is more to
life than material success, food and possessions.

I have Worked Through All Seven Chakras – What Happens Now?

At the end of this chakra journey you may be feeling more grounded, creative, powerful, joyful, expressive, intuitive and inspired. You may feel more comfortable in your body, more at peace with your emotions, with more mental clarity and a deeper spiritual connection. You may also have become aware of all sorts of beautiful chakra colours in your daily life.

If the energy is flowing evenly between all your chakras, so that none of them is underpowered or dominant, then your life will be flowing smoothly, too. I can't guarantee that all of your physical problems, and the tricky people and difficult situations in your life, will magically disappear overnight. But you may feel more confident about handling obstacles and opportunities, and feel optimistic that you are heading in the right direction.

Please do come back to revisit the suggestions and exercises in this book. Life will keep surprising and stretching you, and your chakras will keep evolving, too. Each time you read this book, you will read it slightly differently and some parts may suddenly make sense, or seem particularly relevant. And every time that you connect with your chakras, you will experience them differently, too. Perhaps next time a visualization will feel more intense, as you find the courage to explore deeper, or seem lighter and easier as you let old energy go.

The chakra system is such a useful map; so simple and logical to use, but with an unparalleled depth and subtlety. If you find yourself struggling, check in with your chakras; they can help you to see clearly which aspect of your life needs more support. When you are starting a new project, tune into your chakras; they can help you move forward with clarity and confidence.

The more that you heal, clear, balance and energize your chakras, the easier it will become to manage your energy, and live a fulfilling, joyful life that is an adventure and a journey into the heart of who you really are.

Together, the seven chakras are like the lighthouse of the soul. With good, strong foundations, sturdy walls and a bit of maintenance, they help you to stand tall, so that your light can shine.

Bibliography

ON CHAKRAS

My website: http://georgiacoleridgehealing.com and Instagram: @chakraproject.

Annie Penny's chakra course: https://www.sacredearthtraining.co.uk.

Carter, Hilary H. *The Chakras Made Easy* (Ayni Books, 2013).

Eden, Donna *Energy Medicine: Balancing Your Body's Energies for Optimal Health, Joy, and Vitality*, updated and expanded edition (Tarcher Books, 2008).

Hausauer, Nancy *Chakra Care: Do-It-Yourself Energy Healing for a More Joyful, Loving, Fruitful Life* (CreateSpace Independent Publishing Platform, 2013).

Judith, Anodea *Wheels of Life: The Classic Guide to the Chakra System*, 2nd edition (Llewellyn Publications, 1987).

Judith, Anodea *Eastern Body, Western Mind: Psychology and the Chakra System as a Path to the Self* (Celestial Arts, 2004).

Judith, Anodea and Vega, Selene *The Sevenfold Journey: Reclaiming Mind, Body and Spirit Through the Chakras* (Crossing Press, 1993).

McGeough, Marion *A Beginner's Guide to the Chakras* (CreateSpace Independent Publishing Platform, 2013).

Simpson, Liz *The Book of Chakra Healing*, revised edition (Sterling Publishing, 2013).

White, Ruth *Working with Your Chakras* (Piatkus, 2010).

ON ENERGY, HEALING, PSYCHOLOGY AND MORE

Aron, Elaine N. *The Highly Sensitive Person: How to Thrive When the World Overwhelms You* (Thorsons, 1999).

Bennett Vogt, Stephanie *Your Spacious Self : Clear the Clutter and Discover Who You Are* (Hierophant Publishing, 2012).

Bloom, William *Psychic Protection: Creating Positive Energies for People and Places* (Simon & Schuster, 1970).

Bolte Taylor, Jill *My Stroke of Insight: A Brain Scientist's Personal Journey* (Hodder, 2009).

Brennan, Barbara Ann *Hands of Light: A Guide to Healing Through the Human Energy Field* (Bantam, 1990).

Byrne, Rhonda *The Secret* (Simon & Schuster UK, 2006).

Cain, Susan *Quiet: The Power of Introverts in a World That Can't Stop Talking* (Penguin Books, 2013).

Cuddy, Amy *Presence: Bringing Your Boldest Self to Your Biggest Challenge* (Little, Brown Book Group, 2015).

Emoto, Masaru *The Hidden Messages In Water* (Simon & Schuster UK, 2005).

Garner, Lesley *Everything I've Ever Done That Worked* (Hay House UK, 2010).

Gilbert, Elizabeth *Eat, Pray, Love: One Woman's Search for Everything* (Bloomsbury Publishing, 2006).

Linn, Denise *Past Lives, Present Miracles: The Most*

Empowering Book on Reincarnation You'll Ever Need...
in This Lifetime! (Hay House UK, 2008).

Locke, Amber *Nourish: Vibrant Salads to Relish and
Refresh* (Mitchell Beazley, 2016) and *Savour: Sensational
Soups to Fulfil and Fortify* (Mitchell Beazley, 2017).

Minns, Sue *Soulmates: Understanding the True Gifts of
Intense Encounters* (Hodder, 2005).

Moorjani, Anita *Dying to Be Me: My Journey from Cancer,
to Near Death, to True Healing* (Hay House UK, 2012).

Nhat Hanh, Thich *The Miracle of Mindfulness: The Classic
Guide* (Rider, 2008).

O'Sullivan, Natalia *Do It Yourself Psychic Power: Practical
Tools and Techniques for Awakening Your Natural Gifts*
(Element Books, 2002).

O'Sullivan, Natalia and Graydon, Nicola *The Ancestral
Continuum: Unlock the Secrets of Who You Really Are*
(Simon & Schuster, 2013).

Pollan, Michael *In Defence of Food: The Myth of Nutrition
and the Pleasures of Eating* (Penguin Books, 2008).

Rubin, Gretchen *The Happiness Project* (Harper, 2010).

Samuel, Julia *Grief Works: Stories of Life, Death and
Surviving* (Penguin Life, 2017).

Stone, Hal and Sidra *Embracing Our Selves: the Voice
Dialogue Manual* (Nataraj Publishing, 1988).

Woolger, Roger J. *Other Lives, Other Selves: A Jungian
Psychotherapist Discovers Past Lives* (Thorsons, 1999).

There are also many internet resources – try YouTube
for chakra meditations, chakra yoga (particularly Ingrid
Ballard) and chakra chanting. And blogs on everything
from Sanskrit philosophy to crystals, oils and chakra tea.

Index

Picture Acknowledgements

123RF pro100vector 11. **Alamy Stock Photo** Alex Ramsay 36; Dan Bannister/Tetra Images 65; Maurus Spescha 106. **Getty Images** Alfred Pasieka/Science Photo Library 2; Jodie Griggs 13; Kelly Sillaste 42; Mathias Alvebring/EyeEm 25; PM Images 7; RenataAphotography 126; stilllifephotographer 17; Walker and Walker 14; Zu Sanchez Photography 45. **iStockphoto** Aksiniya_Polyarnaya 19 (1), 19 (2), 19 (3), 19 (4), 19 (5), 19 (6), 19 (7), amenic181 92; Andrew_Mayovskyy 154; AVTG 86; AYakovlev 62; bgfoto 162; borchee 142; Chunumunu 8; davidsorensen 66; debibishop 105; draganab 174; Focus_on_Nature 147; fotoVoyager 46; georgeclerk 124; Gizmo 173; gmutlu 136; Hirurg 61; iamjiere 116; ImpaKPro 144; ithinksky 164; jacquesvandinteren 148; Jasmina007 40; jefunne 158; ksushsh 4; LouisHiemstra 20; Maica 102; MarcinHaber 166; maxkrasnov 121; MRodionova 168; nightman1965 52; Nikada 96, 101; OGphoto 132; Pekic 82; Pete_LD 76; redstallion 32; shaunl 72; Simon Bradfield 140; South_agency 105; SpeedPhoto 112; Sun_Time 26; tjasam 122; twpixels 186; uchar 84; vencavolrab 185; YouraPechkin 170; yupiyan 81 **Jason Ingram** 56. **Octopus Publishing Group** Amber Locke 38, 58, 78, 98, 118, 138, 160.

Acknowledgments

My heart chakra is glowing with gratitude to all the people who inspired this book. Some directly, some indirectly, and I thank you all.

Amaryllis Fraser who first told me I would be a healer, Julia Shepherd at the College of Psychic Studies who first introduced me to chakras, my incredible mentors Natalia and Terry O'Sullivan, Wendy Mandy, Franky Kossy, Jill Purce and Juanita Puddifoot who have taught me how to work with energy (and I'm still learning from you all). Annie Penny for her illuminating in-depth chakra course and our lovely chakra group, Ingrid Ballard, Katy Boughey, Lucinda Bruce, Deborah Everton-Wallace, Jo Kirkpatrick and Helen Taylor, all of whom inspired me to go even deeper into the subject. My daughter Sophie Coleridge for persuading me to put my chakra research on Instagram and teaching me, very patiently, how to post. My Instagram friends – for your inspiring pictures, encouraging words, enthusiasm and humour. Thank you all for supporting me – the material for this book grew and developed under your kind eyes. Ingrid Ballard, who, astonishingly, has taught me yoga for 25 years, and helped me physically experience that beautiful interplay between my body and energy field.

Thank you to my fabulous publisher Kate Adams for spotting the potential of this book, and for bringing it to life – a pretty remarkable journey from crown chakra inspiration to base chakra manifestation! I am grateful to so many people at Octopus and Aster, including publishing director Stephanie Jackson; the talented Yasia Williams and her design team for working so hard to make this book look beautiful; the tactful and clear-brained Polly Poulter and her copy editing team, particularly Mandy Greenfield for working so hard to make the book flow and shine; Ellen Bashford and Ashley Grewal on the publicity team and many more. And I am also grateful to my superwoman agent Caroline Michel, plus Tessa David and the team at Peters Fraser and Dunlop.

Thank you to the angelic Amber Locke for your stunning food photographs.

Thank you particularly to Kate Johnson, Vilma Abella, Zdenek Schaffer and Michaela Schafferova for your kindness and practical support.

Thank you to many other kind and inspiring friends, I can't list you all but I hope you know how much I appreciate you (a lot!).

Thank you to my gorgeous healing clients. It's a huge privilege working with you, and you have all taught me so much about energy, chakras and the glorious complexities of being human.

Thank you to my family – parents, siblings, in-laws and particularly my children Alexander, Freddie, Sophie and Tommy, and my darling husband Nicholas. You light up my life, as well as my chakras.

If you ever see someone glowing like a rainbow, walking through Chelsea, it's probably me thinking about you all.